big science
for little hands

Marvelous
Moving
Things

early childhood science in motion

teacher's guide

Art Credit

Marvelous
Moving
Things

early childhood science in motion

Editor

Mickey Sarquis, Director
Center for Chemistry Education and Terrific Science Programs
Miami University, Middletown, OH

Contributing Authors

Mary Neises, Bauer Elementary School, Miamisburg, OH
Lynn Hogue, Center for Chemistry Education, Miami University, Middletown, OH
Beverly Kutsunai, Kamehameha Elementary School, Honolulu, HI

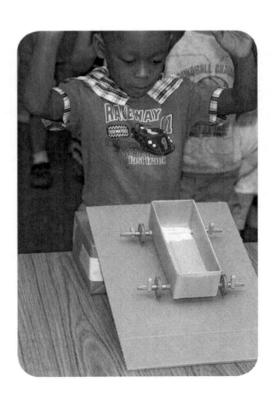

Terrific Science Press
Miami University Middletown
Middletown, Ohio

teacher's guide

Terrific Science Press
Miami University Middletown
4200 East University Boulevard
Middletown, OH 45042
513/727-3269
cce@muohio.edu
www.terrificscience.org

10   9   8   7   6   5   4   3   2   1

This monograph is intended for use by teachers and properly supervised children. The safety reminders associated with experiments and activities in this publication have been compiled from sources believed to be reliable and to represent the best opinions on the subject as of the date of publication. No warranty, guarantee, or representation is made by the authors or by Terrific Science Press as to the correctness or sufficiency of any information herein. Neither the authors nor the publisher assume any responsibility or liability for the use of the information herein, nor can it be assumed that all necessary warnings and precautionary measures are contained in this publication. Other or additional information or measures may be required or desirable because of particular or exceptional conditions or circumstances.

ISBN: 978-1-883822-53-8

The publisher takes no responsibility for the use of any materials or methods described in this monograph, nor for the products thereof. Permission is granted to copy the materials for classroom use.

Contents

Acknowledgments vii

Foreword viii

Using This Book 1

Part 1: Awareness 11

  Awareness 1: Learn Like a Scientist 12

  Awareness 2: Getting Excited About Motion Toys 16

  Awareness 3: How Can We Move These Books? 20

  Awareness 4: All Fall Down 23

  Awareness 5: Go Down the Hill 26

Part 2: Exploration 35

  Exploration 1: Push or Pull 36

  Exploration 2: How Things Move 40

  Exploration 3: Ball Day 44

  Exploration 4: Rolling, Rolling, Round and Round 50

  Exploration 5: Wheel Day 54

  Exploration 6: Moving Fun on the Playground 60

  Exploration 7: Sliding, Sliding, Down and Down 65

  Exploration 8: Going, Going, Up and Down 71

Part 3: Inquiry 77

  Inquiry 1: Ramp It Up 78

  Inquiry 2: Rough Road Ahead 82

  Inquiry 3: Up and Down Seesaw 86

Part 4: Advanced Inquiry 91

  Advanced Inquiry 1: Hill and Loop Challenges 92

  Advanced Inquiry 2: Design a Fun Ramp Ride 96

  Advanced Inquiry 3: I Wonder. 99

Part 5: Application 105

    Application 1: Loaded Question 106

    Application 2: Design Some Fun 110

    Application 3: Bottle Bowling.. 114

Part 6: Motion Across the Curriculum.. 119

    Across the Curriculum 1: Writing to Learn............................. 120

    Across the Curriculum 2: Book Adventures............................ 122

    Across the Curriculum 3: Wheels That Help 124

    Across the Curriculum 4: Fun and Games 126

    Across the Curriculum 5: Motion in Art 128

    Across the Curriculum 6: Safety in Motion 130

Part 7: Science for Young Learners... 133

    Why Early Childhood Science? 134

    Teaching with Learning Cycles 142

    Documenting Learning.. 145

Part 8: All About Motion.. 147

    Our World Is Constantly in Motion.. 148

References 153

Acknowledgments

The authors and editor wish to thank the following individuals who contributed to the development of *Marvelous Moving Things: Early Childhood Science in Motion.*

Terrific Science Press Design and Production Team

Document Production Managers: Amy Stander, Susan Gertz
Production Coordinator: Dot Lyon
Technical Writing: Dot Lyon, Amy Stander
Technical Editing: Amy Stander, Dot Lyon
Production: Anita Winkler, Dot Lyon
Photography: Susan Gertz
Cover Design and Layout: Susan Gertz

Content Specialists, Reviewers, and Testers

Eva Facen, Teacher, Abilities First Early Childhood Learning Center, Middletown, OH

Stacy Francis, Director, Middletown Area Family YMCA Children's Center, Middletown, OH

John Funk, Adjunct Professor, University of Utah, Salt Lake City, UT

Jennifer Kemplin, Director, Abilities First Early Childhood Learning Center, Middletown, OH

Dwight Portman, Visiting Faculty, Miami University, Middletown, OH

Kristiana Reeves, Teacher, Middletown Area Family YMCA Children's Center, Middletown, OH

Teresa Reeves, Teacher, Middletown Area Family YMCA Children's Center, Middletown, OH

Rebecca Shepherd, Teacher, Abilities First Early Childhood Learning Center, Middletown, OH

Foreword

Science is a way for children to explore, discover, and make sense of the world around them. When presented in a way that is meaningful for young minds, early science experiences provide the foundation for a lifetime of science learning both in and beyond school. Science learning is exploring, wondering, and discovering—it is not about memorizing facts.

The goal of the *Big Science for Little Hands* series is to help young children develop an understanding of basic concepts about the physical world and practice basic process skills that fit their level of learning development. How do children develop these concepts and skills? They need repeated personal experiences with materials and events from their everyday world. They explore materials, investigate ideas, and link what they discover with the world around them. *Marvelous Moving Things: Early Childhood Science in Motion* builds skills for a lifetime of learning.

I wish you and the future scientists, leaders, and informed citizens in your care great fun while learning with *Marvelous Moving Things*. Enjoy!

Mickey Sarquis, Director
Terrific Science Programs
Miami University (Ohio)

Using This Book

This section explains the organization of the book and discusses early childhood learning, lesson planning, assessment, acquiring materials for the activities, safety, and setting up the classroom.

Organization of the Book

The book is organized in eight parts.

Parts 1–5 contain 22 activities that address the four phases of the learning cycle: awareness, exploration, inquiry (and advanced inquiry), and application. Each activity is presented in an easy-to-use format. (See pages 8–9 for details on activity format and pages 142–144 for a detailed discussion of learning cycles.)

Part 6: Motion Across the Curriculum contains cross-curricular activities that relate the topic of motion to writing, reading, art, and safety. Teachers may choose to use one or more of these activities before, in between, or after the learning cycle activities.

Part 7: Science for Young Learners contains information on developmentally-appropriate science instruction for young children, why we teach early childhood science, fundamental concepts and process skills, teaching with learning cycles, and documenting learning.

Part 8: All About Motion summarizes motion concepts for teachers. Teachers may want to share the most basic of this information with the children.

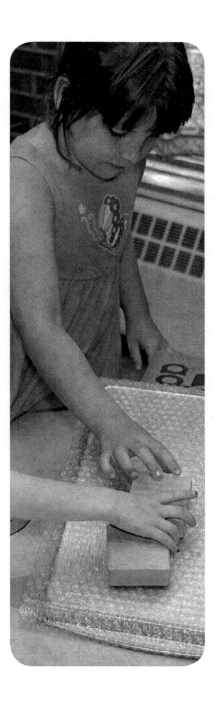

Range of Learners

Because young children are unique individuals who progress at their own pace, they reach the various stages of intellectual, physical, emotional, and social development at different times. Some children will understand all or most of the fundamental concepts about the physical world presented in this book (see page 135 for details), and other children will understand only a few concepts or none at all. However, all will benefit from the hands-on nature of the activities and from exposure to the concepts at this early stage in their education.

Many children will be able to answer the straightforward questions included in the activities, but they are likely to have some difficulty with the inquiry-style questions. With time and practice, children will become more comfortable with inquiry questions. Process and inquiry skills are challenging to young children, but they can learn these skills and build the foundation for a lifetime of science learning. (See **Part 7: Science for Young Learners** for a discussion of inquiry learning and teaching.)

Lesson Planning

Marvelous Moving Things offers a large selection of activities. The activities are organized by the stages of the learning cycle (awareness, exploration, inquiry, and application). Our goal is to provide you with a number of activities at each stage so you can choose what works best for you. For example, teachers wanting to designate one week to learning about motion can select one activity from each phase plus one of the activities in **Part 6: Motion Across the Curriculum**. You do not need to complete activities on consecutive days, although you should present the activities in learning cycle order.

If your class uses centers, you may wish to incorporate **Part 6: Motion Across the Curriculum** activities and other motion experiences as ongoing activities over the duration of the unit. This will provide children with topic enrichment and reinforcement. Center activities might include the following:

Science Center
- Offer tape, scissors, and building materials (such as pieces of cardboard, cardboard tubes, small boxes, pipe cleaners, and plastic cups and bowls) so children can design and build their own motion toys. Ask children to explain their creations to the class.

Art Center
- Do some or all of the art projects in **Across the Curriculum 5: Motion in Art**.
- Offer chalk, washable markers, colored pencils, and paper. Ask children to trace or draw different motion toys.

Math Center
- Offer rulers and tape measures so children can measure the distances that motion toys travel.
- Provide a balance and same-sized weights (such as centimeter/gram cubes or plastic counting bears) so children can weigh a variety of objects. Point out that the balance goes up and down like a seesaw.

Dress-Up/Housekeeping Center
- Do **Across the Curriculum 3: Wheels That Help**. Have the children try sitting and maneuvering in a wheelchair, if available. Have them try to do household chores or put on clothing while sitting in the wheelchair. (Make sure to model appropriate sensitivity to people with disabilities and to convey that wheelchairs are tools and not toys.)

Writing Center

- Offer paper, pencils, and crayons for children to draw or write their own fictional stories about trains, dump trucks, balls, merry-go-rounds, or other things that move.
- Do **Across the Curriculum 1: Writing to Learn**. Children create pictures and stories revealing what they learned about motion.

Assessment

Collecting children's ideas over time is an important feature of ongoing assessment. Examining classroom work helps teachers to identify patterns of learning for individuals as well as groups of children. This process also helps a teacher reflect upon his or her own instructional practice. Teachers can collect samples of work or take photographs of and make notes about children's experiences as they work. These samples, photographs, and notes can be organized into a science journal for each child. (See Documenting Learning on pages 145–146 for a more in-depth discussion of collecting and evaluating evidence of learning.)

As discussed in Teaching with Learning Cycles on page 144, the activities in the application phase of the learning cycle can be used for an assessment at the end of the unit. Teachers may wish to establish evaluation criteria based upon learning objectives such as the following:

- Child learns that scientists ask questions.
- Child gains practice asking questions and applying reason to explain observations.
- Child learns that objects do not move by themselves.
- Child learns that pushing, pulling, and other forces make objects move.
- Child learns that objects move in different ways, such as rolling, spinning, swinging, and going up and down.
- Child learns that wheels make transporting people and objects easier.
- Some children may learn that friction is a force that makes moving objects slow down and stop.

NAEYC Early Childhood Program Accreditation Standards

This book addresses the following preschool and kindergarten National Association for the Education of Young Children (NAEYC) Early Childhood Program Accreditation Standards for science cognitive development under Standard 2: Curriculum.

2.G.02 Children learn key content and principles of science such as structure and property of matter and behavior of materials.

2.G.03 Children use the five senses to observe, explore, and experiment with scientific phenomena.

2.G.04 Children use simple tools to observe objects and scientific phenomena.

2.G.05 Children collect data and represent and document their findings.

2.G.06 Children think, question, and reason about observed and inferred phenomena.

2.G.07 Children discuss scientific concepts in everyday conversation.

2.G.08 Children learn and use scientific terminology and vocabulary associated with the content areas.

National Science Education Standards

This book addresses the following Science Content Standards: K–4.

Science as Inquiry:

Abilities Necessary to Do Scientific Inquiry
- Ask a question about objects, organisms, and events in the environment.
- Plan and conduct a simple investigation.
- Employ simple equipment and tools to gather data and extend the senses.
- Use data to construct a reasonable explanation.
- Communicate investigations and explanations.

Understandings About Scientific Inquiry
- Scientific investigations involve asking and answering a question and comparing the answer with what scientists already know about the world.
- Simple instruments, such as magnifiers, thermometers, and rulers, provide more information than scientists obtain using only their senses.
- Scientists develop explanations using observations (evidence) and what they already know about the world (scientific knowledge). Good explanations are based on evidence from investigations.

Physical Science:

Properties of Objects and Materials

- Objects have many observable properties, including size, weight, shape, color, temperature, and the ability to react with other substances. Those properties can be measured using tools, such as rulers, balances, and thermometers.
- Objects are made of one or more materials, such as paper, wood, and metal. Objects can be described by the properties of the materials from which they are made, and those properties can be used to separate or sort a group of objects or materials.

Position and Motion of Objects

- The position of an object can be described by locating it relative to another object or the background.
- An object's motion can be described by tracing and measuring its position over time.
- The position and motion of objects can be changed by pushing or pulling. The size of the change is related to the strength of the push or pull.

Science and Technology:

Understanding about Science and Technology

- Tools help scientists make better observations, measurements, and equipment for investigations. They help scientists see, measure, and do things that they could not otherwise see, measure, and do.

A Collection of Motion Objects

To begin this unit, you will need to collect a variety of motion objects (toys and other objects that can be moved). The children will be observing these motion objects with their senses and using the objects during hands-on classroom activities. Choose some familiar objects (such as toy cars and balls) as well as some new objects (such as tops and plastic hockey pucks).

Consider the age and experience of your children as you build your collection. Younger children and those building basic experience benefit from a small variety of motion objects. Older children and those with more background may enjoy a wider selection with more subtle differences. As the children become more familiar with motion toy characteristics, add new samples to challenge their learning. Opportunities are included for children and their families to hunt for balls and wheeled toys at home.

Keep in mind that a few activities involve sorting and matching the objects into pairs or groups. Your collection should have enough variety to make these matching activities interesting.

Be Safe

Emphasize safety rules with the children while doing the activities. Remind children not to put objects in their mouths, ears, or near eyes. Children should keep balls, vehicles, and other rolling objects off the floor when not in use. Children should also be reminded of any additional safety issues listed in individual activities.

Setting Up the Learning Environment

Toys and objects that roll, spin, wobble, and move in different ways can be collected and placed in the learning centers throughout the classroom. Placing these objects in the centers allows children to engage, experiment, and explore motion. You'll need other materials that do not move easily (such as blocks, cubes, and boxes) for children to explore for comparison and classifying activities.

Many of the exploration and inquiry activities need a large area where children have space to experiment and interact with the motion objects. Children need a place where balls can roll down ramps and tops can spin freely. If possible, make toys such as wagons, scooters, tricycles or bicycles, and skates available for movement on the playground. Playground equipment will allow children to swing, slide, and balance.

Make and display word cards for children to use when drawing and writing about their explorations. Each card should have a picture of a motion object and the corresponding object name or motion word. Add more word cards to the collection as the unit progresses.

Helpful Hint

Placing objects on trays, paper plates, plastic bins, or aluminum pie pans helps children organize their work space while investigating motion.

Set up the Reading Center with many fiction and nonfiction books and cassettes or CDs about different types of objects that move. The Dress-Up/Housekeeping Center can provide children with materials, props, and opportunities to engage in imaginative simulations of vehicles and other things that move. These learning areas provide fun environments that encourage early learners to understand motion and the world in which they live.

The Social Context

Learning in the early years takes place in a social context. The cooperation and collaboration that begin in these years are important qualities for learners of all ages. Build in opportunities for children to practice these skills. For example, sharing must be practiced in a variety of situations with different people. Encourage children to help each other while working together. They will discover more and gain valuable experience when they listen respectfully to different perspectives and ideas. Fostering these experiences involves a working noise level in your classroom. Working noise does not offend others or interrupt them, but it shows that people are working and developing new ideas. Maintaining a reasonable noise level shows that children respect others who are working in the classroom or building.

Choose materials to encourage social interaction. Some procedures may work better when several children share a task. Sometimes a limited number of materials will encourage children to share with others and set up systems to cooperate. Reflect upon the role social learning has in your classroom and choose how you want to foster this learning in your activities.

Format of Activities

Each activity is presented in an easy-to-use format.

Learning Cycle Phase
Identifies the activity's learning cycle phase. (Details about each phase are discussed in Teaching with Learning Cycles on pages 142–144.)

Activity Title
Identifies the overall goal or theme of the activity.

Activity Introduction
Briefly describes the activity.

Duration
Provides an estimate of the classroom time and group size recommended for the activity.

Purpose
States the skills children will use and develop during the activity.

What You Need
Lists the materials needed to do the activity.

Be Safe
States relevant safety issues to be aware of during the activity.

Helpful Hint Sidebar
Offers teacher tips to enhance or extend the activity.

Process Skill Power Sidebar
Presents information about fundamental process skills that are emphasized in the activity.

Exploration 8:

Going, Going, Up and Down

Children use a balance and playground seesaw to explore up and down motion.

Duration
1 large group session and independent exploration

Purpose
- observe up and down motion
- discover how a balance works to compare weights
- observe cause and effect
- predict and communicate which objects are heavier and which are lighter than a toy animal
- group objects based on how their weights compare to the weight of a toy animal
- apply experiences with a balance when exploring a playground seesaw

What You Need
- index cards
- primary or bucket balance
- one or more toy animals
- ⊙ If you begin the activity by reading a story about an animal on a seesaw, try to choose that type of toy animal.
- objects that weigh the same, more, and less than the toy animal
- designated sorting areas made with yarn, masking tape, hula-hoops, or small rugs (prepared in Getting Ready)
- playground seesaw
- (optional) book about seesaws, such as *Just a Little Bit* (by Ann Tompert)

Be Safe
Be sure children follow normal playground safety rules.

Helpful Hint
The term "weight" is used in this activity since the term "mass" is outside the realm of young children's understanding. (See **Part 8: All About Motion** for further explanation.)

Exploration

Marvelous Moving Things 71

Process Skill Power

"Comparing is a powerful process that can lead to the understanding of many important scientific ideas."

"Organizing is the process of putting objects or phenomena together on the basis of a logical rationale."

Lawrence Lowery, 1992

Getting Ready

- Set up designated sorting areas by either marking out areas of about 3 feet × 3 feet with yarn or tape or laying out objects (such as hula-hoops or rugs). Write or draw on index cards to label the areas "heavier," "same," and "lighter" as shown at left.

Spotlight Vocabulary

- balance (the equipment)
- gravity   • seesaw
- direction words (such as up and down)
- comparison words (such as heavier/lighter and bigger/smaller)

Begin

Sci-Lit Connection

You can begin this activity by reading the class a book about seesaws, such as *Just a Little Bit* (by Ann Tompert).

1. Place a toy animal on one side of a balance. Point out that gravity made that side of the balance go down. Ask the class what they think can be put on the other side of the balance so that the animal will go up.

   Question to guide the inquiry process:
   > *What object or group of objects will be heavier than the animal?*

2. Ask the children to gather objects from the classroom that might make the animal go up. As a class, try different objects and different combinations of objects. Give children a chance to gather and try additional objects. If you have different kinds or sizes of toy animals, you can also have the children determine which of the toy animals is the heaviest.

Seen and heard:
Children said, "That side goes down," "It's the same now," and "It's like a seeter totter."

Exploration

Getting Ready
Provides teachers with instructions for preparing materials prior to the activity (when applicable).

Spotlight Vocabulary
Lists vocabulary words that teachers may want to introduce or reinforce during the activity.

Begin
Lists procedures to begin the activity.

Sci-Lit Connection Sidebar
Offers opportunities for teachers to read books to the class related to the activity.

Guiding Questions
Includes suggested questions to ask children to facilitate the building of process and inquiry skills.

Seen and Heard
Lists examples of children's comments and reactions.

Continue
Lists additional procedures to continue the activity.

What to Look For
Offers children's reactions that indicate understanding of the topic.

Continue

7. Have the children draw themselves riding in a wagon down a hill. Be sure the children draw round wheels. Write brief captions under the pictures based on the artists' own words.

What to Look For

As the children are pulling wheels from the bag, assess if the children can identify the shapes. Also, evaluate the drawings to determine if the children drew round wheels on the wagon. Assess how well the children describe their pictures.

Awareness

Part 1: Awareness

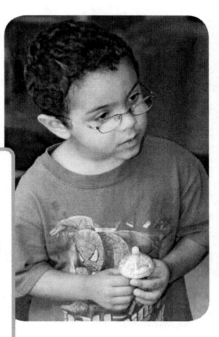

What is the awareness phase?

The awareness phase provides children with experiences to help them develop a broad recognition of and interest in objects, people, events, or concepts.

During awareness, children

- experience,
- awaken curiosity, and
- develop an interest.

The teacher's role is to

- create a rich environment;
- provide opportunities by introducing new objects, people, events, or concepts;
- invite and encourage interest by posing a problem or question;
- respond to children's interest; and
- show interest and enthusiasm.

Awareness 1:
Learn Like a Scientist

Children discover and practice several of the processes and procedures that scientists use to learn about the world around them.

Duration

1 large group session

Purpose

- discover the scientific process
- apply the scientific process to determine how a mystery toy works
- become excited about learning like a scientist

What You Need

- poster board or large piece of paper
- *What Is a Scientist?* (by Barbara Lehn) or similar resource outlining the scientific process
- Cool 'Copter (prepared in Getting Ready) or other unique toy that children probably have not encountered

Getting Ready

- Prepare a class chart as shown at right.
- If you are going to use the Cool 'Copter in step 2, copy the template and follow the directions at the end of this activity.

Spotlight Vocabulary

- question
- draw
- move
- spin
- senses
- record
- drop

> **Helpful Hint**
>
> If *What Is a Scientist?* or a similar resource is unavailable, you can still model the scientific process by doing steps 2–4. Point out that scientists investigate by measuring, making comparisons, sorting, counting, recording what they observe, and doing things over again.

What does this toy do?

> **Helpful Hint**
>
> You can start a "word wall" for all new vocabulary words. Add new words to the wall before doing each new activity. Revisit the wall often.

Begin

1. Read *What Is a Scientist?* to the class. Discuss what is happening in the pictures.

2. Tell the class that you want to be a scientist and ask if the class will help you. Show the class a Cool 'Copter (prepared in Getting Ready). Reread the page stating that scientists ask questions and model the scientific process by telling the class that you wonder, "What does this toy do?"

3. Reread the pages stating that scientists learn by using their senses and observing details. Review the five senses with the class. (See Helpful Hint.) Ask children to use their senses to describe the Cool 'Copter.

   ### Questions to guide the observing process:
   > *What is this toy made of?*
   > *What does this toy look like?...smell like?...sound like?*

   ### Seen and heard:
   Children said, "Folded paper" and "It makes sounds."

4. Reread the pages stating that scientists draw and write down observations. Model this process by drawing a Cool 'Copter on the class chart. Ask children what you should do to make this toy move. While suggestions will vary, begin with methods such as rolling and bouncing the toy. If children have not yet suggested letting the toy drop, guide them to this idea. Try it. Record the whirling motion on the class chart.

   ### Seen and heard:
   Children said, "You can throw it" and "It twirls!"

> **Helpful Hint**
>
> When doing hands-on activities with the children, try to use "I wonder…" statements often to reinforce the way scientists think. Modeling the use of "I wonder…" throughout the unit should make Advanced Inquiry 3: I Wonder… easier for the children to do.

> **Helpful Hint**
>
> Our five senses are:
> • sight
> • hearing
> • touch
> • smell
> • taste

Continue

5. Tell children that they will be learning like scientists by doing many other exciting things. Follow through the remaining pages of the book to review what the children will be doing, including having fun!

What to Look For

Look for children to understand that scientists ask and answer questions. Show enthusiasm as you read the book and talk about all the things children can learn using science.

How to Make a Cool 'Copter

1. Photocopy the template below.

2. Cut along the solid lines as shown in Figure 1. *Do not cut along the dotted lines.*

3. Fold the bottom flaps in as shown in Figure 2. Tape the flaps in place.

4. Fold the top flaps down along the dotted line to opposite sides of the toy as shown in Figure 3.

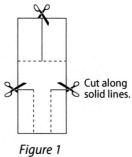

Cut along solid lines.

Figure 1

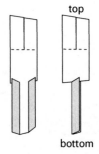

top

bottom

Figure 2

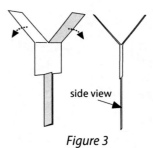

side view

Figure 3

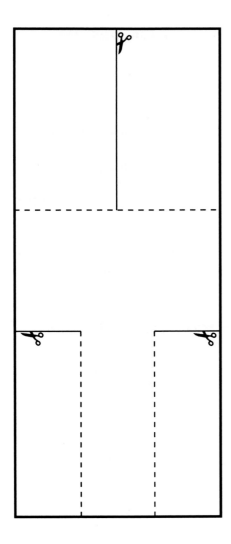

Awareness 2:
Getting Excited About Motion Toys

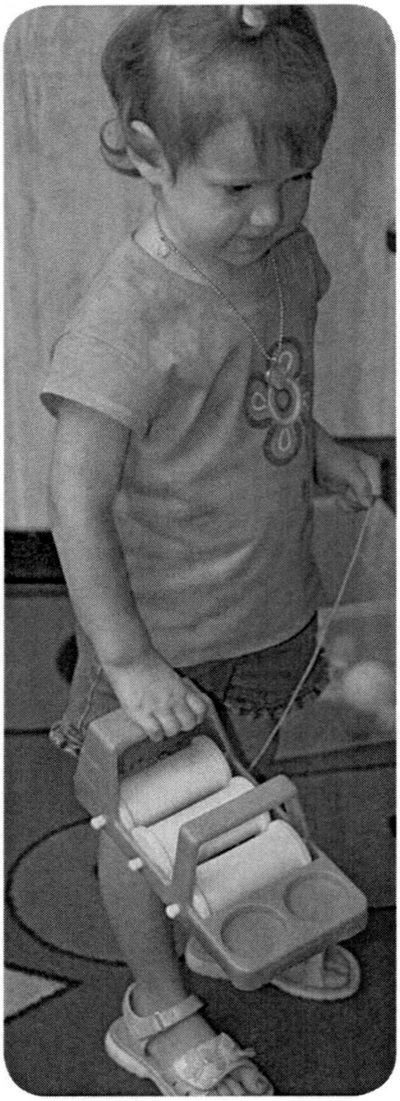

Children collect objects in the classroom and, by sharing ideas, discover that many things can *be manipulated to move in certain ways.*

Duration

1 large group session and independent exploration

Purpose

- use senses to explore how objects can be moved
- communicate ideas to the class
- use proper listening and sharing skills in a group setting

What You Need

- poster board or large piece of paper
- index cards
- wide variety of motion objects that can be manipulated and moved
- ☞ *Choose objects that roll (such as toy cars and balls), spin (such as tops and yo-yos), and slide (such as blocks and hockey pucks). Make sure that the objects are exciting and new for the children in order to pique interest and excitement.*

Be Safe

Keep safety in mind when choosing objects for exploration.

Getting Ready

- Prepare a class chart as shown at left. Be sure to allow room in the last column for index cards.
- Place the motion objects in various centers throughout the classroom.

Example of class chart

Object	Force to make object move	Movement

index cards go here

- Prepare index cards that show the motion of objects you placed around the classroom. (See examples below.)

Spotlight Vocabulary

- object   • move
- motion words (such as roll, spin, and slide)
- force words (such as push, pull, turn, twist, and kick)

Begin

1. After giving the class sufficient time for free exploration with the new objects located throughout the classroom, ask each child to pick one object. Have the children sit in a circle with their chosen objects placed in front of them.

2. Choose an interesting motion object from the classroom to model how you want each child to share with the class. Say what the object is, explain what you have to do to make the object move, and tell how the object moves (for example, rolls, spins, or slides). Demonstrate by making the object move.

Continue

3. Ask one child to stand and share his or her object with the class just as you did in step 2. While the child demonstrates the object's movement, prompt the child by asking questions or providing comments. This encouragement helps the child focus on what information should be shared. Summarize what the child says on a class chart. Attach index cards (prepared in Getting Ready) where appropriate to show the movement of toys. (See example at left.)

Object	Force to make object move	Movement	
car	push	roll	
'copter	drop (gravity)	spin	
block	push	slide	
ball	push	roll	
ball	drop (gravity)	bounce	
top	twist	spin	

Questions to guide the sharing:

> *What is your object?*

> *What do you need to do to make the object move?*

> *How does the object move? Does it roll, spin, slide...?*

Seen and heard:

Children said, "I pushed the car and it moved," "The spinner [top] is going around," and "It slides like a worm."

4. Repeat step 3 for the remaining children.

5. Review with the class what they observed and explored regarding the motion of selected objects. Have the children return their objects to the proper places in the room.

What to Look For

Evaluate whether the children comprehend descriptive motion words such as roll, spin, and slide. Show interest and excitement throughout the unit as children discover more about motion and force.

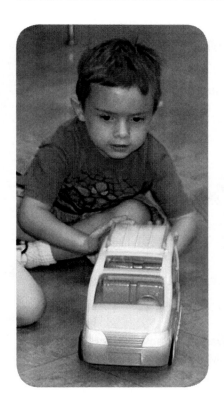

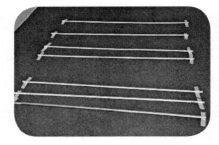

Awareness 3:
How Can We Move These Books?

While involved in this problem-solving activity, children work to discover a solution and become excited about the concept of motion.

Duration

1 large group session and independent exploration

Purpose

- work with others to solve a problem
- evaluate and communicate solutions
- discover that wheels make transporting objects easier
- compare rolling over smooth surfaces and rolling over bumpy surfaces

What You Need

- large stack of books
- ☞ *Make sure that individual books are not too heavy for children to lift.*
- wagon
- box that fits in the wagon and is large enough to hold a stack of books
- objects to make a bumpy path (such as dowel rods and carpet pieces)
- masking tape
- (optional) book about using a wagon to move objects, such as *The Magic School Bus: Liz on the Move* (by Tracey West)
- (optional) shopping bags, toy strollers, or other objects used to carry items

Be Safe

Supervise the moving of books in the box and wagon. Make sure the children pull the wagon safely.

Getting Ready

- Set up a bumpy path to the Reading Center by taping dowel rods or carpet pieces to the floor. (You can put nonbreakable objects under the carpet pieces to make the path even bumpier.)

Dowel rods taped to the floor make a bumpy path.

- Test the bumpy path to make sure children can pull a wagon full of books over it.
- Place a large stack of books across the room from the Reading Center. Be sure to place the wagon and box nearby so children will have visual clues while coming up with solutions to the problem.

Spotlight Vocabulary

- easiest
- force words (such as carry, drag, lift, push, and pull)
- smooth   • bumpy

Begin

1. Introduce the problem by telling children that you need to move a large stack of books from one area over to the Reading Center. Ask the children to come up with the easiest way to move the books. Through questions and discussion, guide the children to suggest putting the books in a box to carry or push. Also, guide the children to suggest moving the books in a wagon over the smooth floor.

Sci-Lit Connection

You can begin this activity by reading the class a book about using a wagon to move objects, such as *The Magic School Bus: Liz on the Move* (by Tracey West).

2. Have some children carry the books in their arms, some children carry or push the books in a box, and some children move the books in the wagon.

3. Have children switch roles and repeat step 2 until each child experiences all methods of transporting the books. Discuss which method of moving the books is easiest.

Continue

4. Present the children with a testable question, then let them experiment. This process will reinforce the lesson learned in **Awareness 1: Learn Like a Scientist**. For example, ask the children if it is easier to pull a wagon over a smooth path or a bumpy path. To find the answer, have the children experiment with pulling the wagon over the smooth floor and then pulling the wagon over a bumpy path (set up in Getting Ready). Children should discover that it is easier to roll over a smooth path.

5. Let the children continue exploring with the box, wagon, and bumpy path. You can also add shopping bags, toy strollers, and other things that help us move objects.

What to Look For

Watch for children to relate past experiences as they make suggestions on how to move the books. Encourage enthusiasm and respect for others as the class works together to solve the problem.

Awareness 4:
All Fall Down

Children explore falling objects.

Duration

1 large group session and independent exploration

Purpose

- observe objects falling

What You Need

- different types of objects that don't bounce or roll (such as bean bags, blocks, and stuffed animals)

Spotlight Vocabulary

- hold
- let go
- drop
- fall
- gravity
- force words (such as lift and pull)
- direction words (such as up and down)

Begin

1. Give each child an object. Have the children observe what happens when they hold their objects above the floor and then let go. Discuss the results.

   Questions to guide the discussion:
   > *What happened when you let go of the object?*
   > *Where did the object land?*
   > *Will the object fall in the same way next time you drop it? Try it.*

   Seen and heard:
   Children said, "It fell down" and "It dropped and was loud."

2. Have children trade objects and repeat step 1.

3. Ask the children to summarize what happened to the objects when let go. Encourage the children to describe how the objects moved. Point out that the objects didn't just stay where they were after children let go. Mention that something called gravity made the objects fall to the floor.

Continue

4. Ask children to jump in the air and observe what happens. Discuss the results. Point out that the children pushed with their legs to jump up off the floor, but they didn't have to do anything to come back down. Mention that gravity made them fall back down to the floor.

Question to guide the discussion:
> *Why didn't you stay in the air after you jumped up?*

Seen and heard:

A child said, "Gravity is stuff that makes you stay on the ground."

5. Make the objects available to the children for free exploration.

What to Look For

Look for children to understand that most objects fall to the floor when dropped.

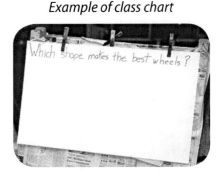

Awareness 5:
Go Down the Hill

Children observe that the shape of the wheels on a car make a difference in how the car goes down a hill.

Duration

1 large group session and independent exploration

Purpose

- observe how a car goes downhill in different ways using different-shaped wheels
- recognize and match shapes (circle, square, triangle, and rectangle)
- work together to decide which wheel shape works best

What You Need

- poster board or large piece of paper
- toy car with four types of removable wheels
- 🖐 *Directions on how to make a car with removable wheels are provided at the end of this activity.*
- ramp
- 🖐 *You can prop up stiff cardboard or a wooden board with books, blocks, or boxes.*
- brown paper grocery bag
- 🖐 *Children need to be able to put both hands in the bag and not see through the sides. As an alternative, cut a 2-foot section out of an unwanted pant leg or shirt sleeve to make a tube.*
- paper and drawing materials
- (optional) book about going downhill in a car or wagon, such as *The Lazy Bear* (by Brian Wildsmith)

Example of class chart

Getting Ready

- Prepare a class chart as shown at left.
- Make a car with removable wheels. (You can follow the directions at the end of this activity.) Remove all wheels for step 1 of the classroom procedure.
- Prepare all the wheel shapes.
- Set up a ramp for the toy car.

- Cut about 5 inches off the top of the brown paper grocery bag so children can reach the bottom of the bag. Put all the wheels in the bag.

Spotlight Vocabulary
- wheel
- down
- roll
- ramp
- shape
- slide
- shape words (such as square, rectangle, triangle, and circle)

Sci-Lit Connection

You can begin this activity by reading the class a book about going downhill in a car or wagon, such as *The Lazy Bear* (by Brian Wildsmith).

Begin

1. Show the class a toy car that is missing its wheels. Ask children to predict what would happen if the car was released at the top of a ramp. Try it. Point out that the car doesn't roll. If the car slides down the ramp, point that out too. Ask the children how the car can be changed to make it go down the ramp more easily.

2. Reach in the bag and pull out a wheel other than a round wheel. Ask the class to identify the shape of the wheel (rectangle, triangle, or square). Draw the shape on the class chart.

3. Have a child reach into the bag with both hands (without looking inside), feel the wheels, and pull out a wheel that matches the shape of the wheel already selected. Repeat with different children until all four wheels are found.

Helpful Hint

Children collect more information when they feel the wheels in the bag with both hands.

4. Place the four wheels gathered in steps 2 and 3 on the car. Ask children to predict what will happen when the car is released at the top of the ramp. Try it. Discuss how the car moves down the ramp.

Questions to guide the predicting process:
> *What will happen when this car goes down the ramp?*

Seen and heard:
Children said, "It's going to slide or roll" and "It's going to stay 'cause it's not a circle."

5. Repeat steps 2–4 with different volunteers and different wheel shapes, guiding children to save the round wheels for last.

6. Ask a child to go to the chart and circle the wheel shape that works best. Make the toy car, wheels, and ramp available to the children for further exploration.

Continue

7. Have the children draw themselves riding in a wagon down a hill. Be sure the children draw round wheels. Write brief captions under the pictures based on the artists' own words.

What to Look For

As the children are pulling wheels from the bag, assess if the children can identify the shapes. Also, evaluate the drawings to determine if the children drew round wheels on the wagon. Assess how well the children describe their pictures.

Have More Fun

☐ After discussing safety tips about kids in wagons, give each child a short and safe ride in the real wagon down a hill or ramp. (Use caution when giving rides to the children in a real wagon. Be sure that the hill children ride down is small and appropriate for the age group.) Point out that the wheels on the wagon are round. Ask the children what they think would happen if the wheels were switched to a different shape.

How to Make a Car with Removable Wheels

1. Cut around a cereal box about 4 inches from the bottom. Discard the top of the box. Cut 2 inches down the four corners of the remaining portion of the box. Fold and tape each side down as shown below.

2. As shown below, use scissors to poke four holes in the long sides of the box to make room for the axles.

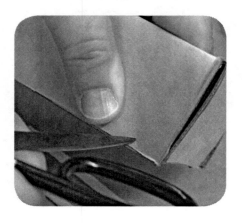

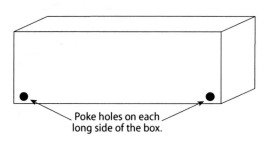

Poke holes on each long side of the box.

3. Use garden pruners to cut two axles from a wooden dowel. To figure out the proper axle length, measure the width of the box and add 4 inches.

🍃 *As an alternative to wooden dowels and wheels, you can use rods and wheels from toy building sets such as K'NEX®.*

4. Insert each axle through the holes in the box and tape down as shown below.

5. Assemble the round wheels using either method shown below. Make sure the round wheels spin freely.

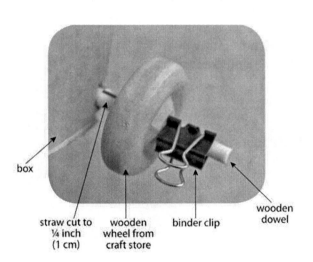

box

straw cut to
¼ inch
(1 cm)

wooden
wheel from
craft store

binder clip

wooden
dowel

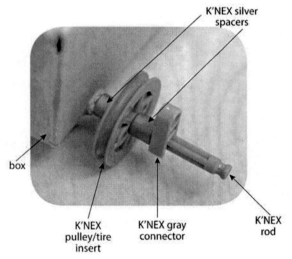

K'NEX silver
spacers

box

K'NEX
pulley/tire
insert

K'NEX gray
connector

K'NEX
rod

6. Make sets of wheels that are rectangles, triangles, and squares. Wheels should be sized to fit the toy car and can be made of wood, Styrofoam® meat trays, clay, stiff cardboard, or any other sturdy material. (Sand wooden wheels to prevent splinters.)

7. Practice removing the round wheels and attaching the different-shaped wheels. End by removing all wheels for step 1 of the classroom procedure.

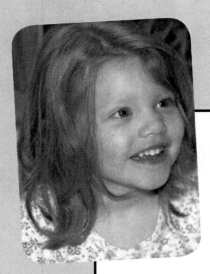

Stop and Reflect

Review with the children what scientists do to discover and learn. Review the many objects children explored that can be manipulated to move in certain ways.

Guide the reflection process by asking
- What can you do to work like a scientist?
- What have you noticed about motion?
- What could we do to find out more about motion?

Encourage children to use their own words to describe the process skills they use to work like scientists. For example, a child may say that he or she "looks" or "touches" rather than "observes." Tell children that they will be working like scientists to learn lots more about motion.

What to look for
Children should be aware of and excited about working like scientists to learn more about motion.

Helpful hint
Some children are challenged by working in a large group situation and may be too shy to contribute. You can meet with small groups and individuals to help children understand that participating and contributing their ideas is an important expectation.

Part 2: Exploration

What is the exploration phase?

The exploration phase enables children to construct personal meaning through sensory experiences with objects, people, events, or concepts.

During exploration, children

- observe and explore materials,
- collect information, and
- construct their own understandings and meanings from their experiences.

The teacher's role is to

- facilitate, support, and enhance exploration;
- ask open-ended questions;
- respect children's thinking and rule systems;
- allow for constructive error; and
- model ways to organize information from experiences.

Exploration 1:
Push or Pull

Children explore the forces of push and pull.

Duration
1 large group session and independent exploration

Purpose
- observe that objects do not move by themselves
- explore how objects can be pushed and pulled

What You Need
- wheeled toy
- wagon
- toys that can be pushed or pulled
- swing

- 🖐 *If your playground does not have a swing, you can use an infant swing with a doll or stuffed animal as a passenger. You can also build a swing from a toy building set or dowel rods and string as shown at right.*

- (optional) book about pushing and pulling, such as *Push and Pull* (by Susan Canizares and Betsey Chessen)

Be Safe
Be sure that children remain at safe distances from the path of a playground swing.

Spotlight Vocabulary
- force
- move
- motion words (such as swing and roll)
- force words (such as push and pull)

Begin

1. Sit with the children in a circle. Place a wheeled toy on the floor in front of you. Tell the class that you want to make the toy move without touching it. Try commanding the toy to move. Ask the children to chime in. Summarize by saying that the toy won't move unless something is done to it. A force is needed to make the toy move.

2. Explain that pushing is a force. Roll the toy across the circle to one of the children as you say, "I push the car and it rolls." Ask that child to repeat the process with another child in the circle. Having the whole class chant the sentence "I push the car and it rolls" will reinforce the learning.

3. Demonstrate the words "push" and "pull" while taking the class to the playground with a wagon full of push and pull toys. Pull the wagon as the class leaves for the playground. Be sure to point out that you are pulling the wagon. Along the way, stop and ask if the wagon could be moved without pulling it. Prompt the children to suggest pushing the wagon, then move the wagon that way to the playground.

Continue

4. On the playground, children should sit at a safe distance from an empty swing. Do not touch the swing but instead look at the swing and yell, "Move, swing." Also have the children yell at the swing to tell it to move. The swing will not move (unless it is a very windy day and the wind makes it move). The class should discuss that an object will not move on its own. Remind the class that someone or something has to make the swing move. A force is needed to make an object move. A force is a push or pull.

5. Push the empty swing and let go. Ask the children what happened.

Questions to guide the observing process:

> *How did I make the swing move?*

> *What did I do to the swing to make it move?*

Seen and heard:

Children said, "You pushed it" and "Pushing makes it go higher."

6. Grab the swing to stop it from swinging, and then pull the empty swing back and let go. Ask the children what happened.

Questions to guide the observing process:

> *How did I make the swing move?*

> *What did I do to the swing to make it move?*

Seen and heard:

Children said, "You pulled the swing back" and "You pulled the other way."

7. Stop the swing. Without releasing the swing, push it and say "I can push the swing." Now pull the swing back and say, "I can pull the swing." Repeat several times. Next, push and pull the swing several times with different children sitting in the swing.

8. Demonstrate pushing and pulling with the toys you brought in the wagon. Be sure to point out that you are using a force to move the toys. Have the children try pushing and pulling the toys.

What to Look For

Look for understanding that objects don't move by themselves. Assess whether children correctly use the force words push and pull.

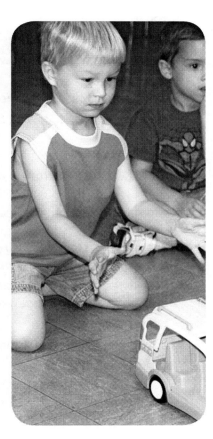

Sci-Lit Connection

You can further explore pushing and pulling by reading a book, such as *Push and Pull* (by Susan Canizares and Betsey Chessen).

Let's Sing

Move It
(sung to the tune of Frére Jacque)

Move it, move it

Move it, move it

Make it move

Make it move

Push the toy to move it

Pull the toy to move it

Now it moves

Now it moves

Exploration 2:
How Things Move

Children sort objects by how the objects can be moved and then play games to reinforce what they have learned.

Duration

1 large group session

Purpose

- compare and sort objects by how they can be moved
- match objects based on how they can be moved
- communicate observations about object movement by using words and acting out the motions
- play games while following the rules and using good manners

What You Need

- class chart from **Awareness 2: Getting Excited About Motion Toys**
- wide variety of motion objects that can be manipulated and moved
- ☞ *Choose objects that roll (such as toy cars and balls), spin (such as tops and yo-yos), and slide (such as blocks and hockey pucks).*
- designated sorting areas made with yarn, masking tape, hula-hoops, or small rugs (prepared in Getting Ready)
- index cards
- assortment of objects for the Motion Matching game (prepared in Getting Ready)
- box to hold the objects for the Motion Matching game

Getting Ready

- Place motion objects in various centers throughout the classroom.
- Set up designated sorting areas as shown at left by either marking out areas of about 3 feet × 3 feet with yarn or tape or laying out objects (such as hula-hoops or rugs).

- For the Motion Matching game, gather a set of objects that can be matched into pairs based on type of motion. Place the objects in a box.

Spotlight Vocabulary
- sort
- group
- match
- act out
- motion words (such as spin, slide, and roll)
- force words (such as push, pull, turn, twist, and lift)

Helpful Hint

Keep the objects used in the games simple and child-friendly. Plan out combinations for the Motion Matching game so that everyone has someone to match with. Many toys of the same category can be used, but a child can only match with one other child at a time.

Begin

1. Explain what "sort" and "group" mean by going through some examples with the class. Tell the children you want to sort the class into two groups. Ask the girls to go to one side of the room and the boys to go to the other side.

2. Gather the class together again. Tell them that now you want to sort the class based on type of shirt. For example, ask the class to split into those wearing striped shirts and those wearing shirts without stripes.

3. Have the class gather together again. Without the children knowing the criteria of your grouping, divide the class into three or more groups based on something else they are wearing (for example, long pants, short pants, and skirts/dresses). See if the class can guess why you grouped them the way that you did.

4. Use the class chart created in **Awareness 2: Getting Excited About Motion Toys** to review ways in which objects can be moved. Be sure to include the force needed to make the object move. For example, push a ball to make it roll and twist a top to make it spin. Point out that many areas (centers) in the room contain objects that can be moved. Have each child choose an object from the room and then sit in a circle on the floor with the object in front of him or her. If the children have not selected objects representing some of the motions you'd like to explore with the class, gather objects representing the missing motions and place them in front of you.

Matching two objects that can slide

5. Call out a type of motion such as "rolling" and have the children hold up the objects that roll. Ask the children to place their rolling objects in one of the designated sorting areas. Ask the children if any of the objects in front of you could be rolled. If so, add them to the designated area. Write "roll" on an index card and place the card in the appropriate sorting area.

6. Repeat step 5 with other motions (such as spin and slide) until all the objects are sorted. Be open to the possibility that children will move some objects in unexpected ways, such as spinning a ball or sliding a toy cylinder.

Continue

7. Now have the children practice matching by playing the Motion Matching game. Give each child one of the objects you selected in Getting Ready. Ask children to place the objects in front of them on the floor so that everyone can see.

8. Call on someone to hold up his or her object and tell the class how the object can move. Ask that person to find someone with an object that matches this movement. For example, a ball that rolls can match with a fire truck that rolls. Accept any answer that makes sense and demonstrates an understanding of matching movements.

Questions to guide the comparing process:

> *How does your toy move? How does his or her toy move?*

> *Do these two toys move in the same way?*

Seen and heard:

Children said, "Mine rolls and his rolls" and "We have wheels."

9. On subsequent days, allow children to sort different collections of objects while working in small groups or individually. Ask children to explain their sorting criteria.

What to Look For

Assess whether the children are able to sort, match, and describe the different objects by how they move. Do the children understand that different objects move in different ways? Do children realize that something has to be done to the objects in order to make them move?

Be sure to let the children organize the objects using their own classification systems; this will show you where they are in the development of sorting skills. The objective of this activity is for children to have a reason for the match based on any characteristic they can observe and explain. Offer more opportunities to sort as the children continue to explore objects. Children can show you what they are learning and will become more comfortable as they practice. Take notes and check their continuing development of this concept during the unit.

Have More Fun

☐ Have children play Motion Charades. Collect all the objects from step 7 and put them in a box. Show one child an object from the box without the other children seeing the object. Ask the child to act out the movement of the object while the other children try to guess the object. Repeat with other volunteers.

Exploration 3:
Ball Day

Children bring balls from home to explore how balls move in different situations and over different surfaces.

Duration

1 large group session

Purpose

- observe that objects do not move by themselves
- communicate about balls in front of the class
- compare and sort balls based on physical characteristics and how the balls can be moved
- communicate observations about how balls move differently on different surfaces
- dictate and illustrate sentences that summarize the activity

What You Need

- letter to parents (sample provided at end of activity)
- poster board or large piece of paper
- scissors
- sports ball for teacher demonstration
- balls from home
- designated sorting areas made with yarn, masking tape, hula-hoops, or small rugs (prepared in Getting Ready)
- slide or ramp
- grassy area
- blacktop or cement area
- different surfaces having a variety of textures (such as carpet, tiled floors, and tabletops)
- drawing paper and drawing materials
- (optional) string for measuring balls
- (optional) book about balls, such as *Froggy Plays Soccer* (by Jonathan London) or *Stop That Ball* (by Mike McClintock)
- (optional) digital camera and printer

Be Safe

Remind children to handle balls carefully, especially indoors. Children should not throw or kick balls at people (especially not at their heads). Remind children not to put balls in their mouths.

Helpful Hint

Try to have a collection of balls for the classroom that can be used throughout the study of motion. Include different kinds of balls such as cotton balls, tennis balls, and Ping-Pong balls.

Getting Ready

- Send letters home prior to Ball Day.
- Prepare a class chart as shown at right.
- Set up designated sorting areas by either marking out areas of about 3 feet × 3 feet with yarn or tape or laying out objects (such as hula-hoops or rugs).
- If a slide is not available, set up a ramp either inside or outside.
- Cut paper into large circles for step 11.

Spotlight Vocabulary

- stay still
- motionless
- move
- friction
- catch
- throw
- texture words (such as smooth, bumpy, and rough)
- speed words (such as slow and fast)
- motion words (such as roll and spin)
- force words (such as kick, hit, lift, and push)

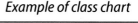

Example of class chart

What can we do with balls?

Begin

1. Lay a sports ball on the table or floor and pretend to try to get it to move by looking at it and telling it to move (but don't touch it). Ask the class what needs to be done to make the ball move. Emphasize that an object will stay still (motionless) unless a force is used to move the object (such as pushing, pulling, or lifting). Use descriptive words or phrases to explain how you use the sports ball. For example, "I can kick my black-and-white soccer ball when I play soccer" or "I like to hit my small white golf ball with a golf club when I play golf with my friends."

2. Have children sit in a circle with the balls they brought from home. Ask the children to place the balls in front of them without touching the balls. Ask each child to share a story about his or her ball similar to the one you shared about the sports ball. Then have the child do something to the ball to make it move.

   Questions to guide the sharing process:

   > *When do you use your ball?*

   > *How do you make your ball move?*

Helpful Hint

Be sure to have extra balls available in case someone forgets to bring a toy from home.

Sci-Lit Connection

You can begin this activity by reading the class a book about balls, such as *Froggy Plays Soccer* (by Jonathan London) or *Stop That Ball* (by Mike McClintock).

Seen and heard:

Children said, "I throw it to my dad," "I kick it," and "I dropped it and it bounced."

3. Decide as a class how to sort the balls (such as by kind of ball, size, or color), then sort the balls into the designated sorting areas. Analyze the results by asking the children questions.

Questions to guide the sorting and comparing process:
> *Which kind of ball do we have the most of?*
> *Which kind of ball do we have the least of?*
> *How many soccer balls do we have?*
> *Which kind of ball has three in its group?*
> *How many red balls do we have?*

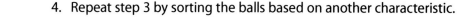

4. Repeat step 3 by sorting the balls based on another characteristic.

5. Ask children to line up their balls by size from largest ball to smallest ball.

6. With the help of the class, make a list on a class chart of all the things you can do with a ball. As the children make suggestions, ask different children to demonstrate the actions. Display the class chart in the classroom.

Helpful Hint

Balls that seem to be the same size can be measured around the largest part with string. The strings can be compared to see which ball is the largest.

Continue

7. Play Follow the Leader by taking children and their balls on a trip around the school. Take your sports ball from step 1 and lead the children in the classroom and outside on the playground to discover how their balls roll, spin, and move on different areas and surfaces. Each ball should be rolled down the slide or ramp (an inclined plane).

8. End the Follow the Leader game on the grass. Ask the children to gather around and observe. Have the children do something to make their balls move only a short distance. Ask them what they did. Next ask the children to move their balls a long distance. Ask them what they had to do to make their balls go further. Point out that pushing (rolling or kicking) harder on a ball makes the ball go further.

9. Release a large ball down a ramp and across the grass. Point out that the ball rolls, slows down, then stops. Ask the children to observe how far the ball travels. Next, release the same ball down the ramp and across blacktop or cement. Point out that this time the ball goes further, but still slows down and stops.

Questions to guide the observing process:
> *Does the ball go slower or faster on the blacktop than on the grass?*
> *Why does the ball move differently over the different surfaces?*
> *Why does the ball slow down and then stop?*

Seen and heard:
Children said, "Faster on the blacktop" and "It gets stuck."

10. Have the children try rolling their balls on grass and on blacktop or cement. Encourage the children to roll their balls the same way each time. The children can then take the balls inside the school to roll on carpet, tiled floor, or a tabletop. Encourage them to describe and compare how the balls move and roll on each of the surfaces. Mention that something called friction makes the ball and the floor or tabletop rub together and makes the ball move differently.

11. Have each child draw a picture on a round ball-shaped paper about one thing they did during Ball Day. Write a brief caption under the picture based on the artist's own words. You can also photograph each child with their ball to make additional pages. Assemble pages into a class book. Remember to create a title page and include children's names as authors.

What to Look For

The children should be realizing that a ball does not move on its own. A ball has to be pushed, pulled, or lifted in order for it to move. Children should notice that balls come in different colors, sizes, and materials and that balls are used for different things. The children should be using descriptive words to explain what their ball looks like and what can be done with the ball. They should also be discovering that their ball will move differently in different places and on different surfaces.

big science
for little hands

Dear Parents:

As part of our science explorations, we are studying objects and how we can make them move. We've already looked at different kinds of objects in our classroom, but now we would like to have a Ball Day to learn more.

Please join your child in a search for balls at home. There are many kinds of balls. Hunt carefully and collect them to examine and compare. Once you have finished hunting for balls, encourage your child to observe the balls and tell you something about what he or she observes. You might want to assist in this observation by asking several questions: What does this ball look like? What does it feel like? What can this ball be used for? How are the balls the same? How are they different?

Have your child choose one favorite ball to bring to school. Put your child's name on the ball so it won't get lost.

We will be sharing our balls in class on Ball Day. Please help your child to remember to bring his or her ball to school on _____. Thank you for your help. Have fun!

Sincerely,

Exploration 4:
Rolling, Rolling, Round and Round

Children explore rolling marbles, balls, and other objects down ramps and then sort the objects based on physical characteristics.

Duration

1 large group session and independent exploration

Purpose

- observe physical characteristics of objects to reveal similarities and differences
- explore how objects move down a ramp
- compare and sort objects based on physical characteristics and rolling ability

What You Need

- different types and sizes of balls and marbles
- ramp
- ☞ *You can prop up stiff cardboard or a wooden board with books or blocks.*
- shoebox lid or wagon
- assortment of objects that will roll (such as toy vehicles, round fruit, cylindrical cans, rolling pins, and round lids)
- designated sorting areas made with yarn, masking tape, hula-hoops, or small rugs (prepared in Getting Ready)
- (optional) book about balls or other objects rolling down hills, such as *Little Pig's Bouncy Ball* (by Alan Baron)
- (optional) book about spheres, such as *What Is Round?* (by Rebecca Kai Dotlich)

Be Safe

Remind children not to put marbles or other small objects in their mouths.

Getting Ready

- Place rolling objects in various centers throughout the classroom.

- Set up a ramp.
- Gather a set of objects that includes a sphere, cylinder, wheeled vehicle, and something that doesn't roll. This set will assure that all sorting categories are represented in step 6.
- Set up designated sorting areas by either marking out areas of about 3 feet × 3 feet with yarn or tape or laying out objects (such as hula-hoops or rugs).

Spotlight Vocabulary
- ramp
- roll
- gravity
- direction words (such as up and down)
- shape words (such as round and cylinder)
- size words (such as big, little, and small)
- color words (such as red, blue, and green)
- descriptive words (such as heavy, smooth, and rubbery)
- speed words (such as slow and fast)

Begin

1. Discuss Ball Day and all the different kinds of balls that children brought to school. Review what happened when the balls were put at the top of the slide (ramp) and released. Roll different sizes and kinds of balls down a ramp. Tell the children that gravity is pulling the balls down the ramp. Ask children to observe how different kinds of balls roll differently.

2. Introduce the class to marbles. (Remind children not to put marbles in their mouths.) Show the class different sizes and colors of marbles and balls. Ask the class to discuss and compare what is the same (for example, the shapes) and what is different (for example, the weights and sizes) about the marbles and balls.

> ### Sci-Lit Connection
> You can begin this activity by reading the class a book about balls or other objects rolling down hills, such as *Little Pig's Bouncy Ball* (by Alan Baron).

Continue

3. Put the marbles in a shoe box lid. Move the lid and ask the children to observe the behavior of the marbles. You can also put the marbles in a wagon to observe how the marbles move when the wagon moves.

4. Explore with the children how the marbles move down the ramp.

5. Tell the children that you wonder what else can roll and move down a ramp like marbles and balls. Have the children gather other things around the room that they want to try on the ramp. Allow each child to try his or her objects on the ramp to see if the objects roll down.

6. Show the class your collection of objects (gathered in Getting Ready). One by one, ask the children to predict how each object will move down the ramp, then try it.

7. Sort all the objects into the designated sorting areas. Objects should be grouped into spheres (such as marbles and balls), objects that have wheels (such as cars and trucks), objects in the shape of cylinders (such as cans and rolling pins), and objects that do not roll.

8. Make the objects and ramp available for free exploration.

Sci-Lit Connection

You can end this activity by reading a book about spheres, such as *What Is Round?* (by Rebecca Kai Dotlich).

What to Look For

The children need to see a similarity between balls, marbles, cans, and toys with wheels. (These objects can roll.) The sorting step lets the children also see the differences between these rolling objects.

Exploration 5:
Wheel Day

Children bring wheeled toys from home to observe, compare, and explore wheels in different situations and over different surfaces.

Duration
1 large group session and additional sessions as time permits

Purpose
- communicate about wheeled toys in front of the class
- observe that wheels make transporting objects easier
- communicate observations about how wheeled toys move differently on different surfaces
- explore wheels through art, reading, sensory experiences, and free play

What You Need
- letter to parents (sample provided at end of activity)
- index cards and drawing materials
- supplies for making graphs, such as masking tape, yarn, index cards, poster board, and construction paper
- wheeled toys from home
- big box of blocks
- wagon
- 2 toy cars (one with its wheels removed)
- slide or ramp
- grassy area
- blacktop or cement area
- different surfaces having a variety of textures (such as carpet, tiled floors, and tabletops)
- (optional) book about wheels, such as *Wheels!* (by Annie Cobb) or *Wheel Away!* (by Dayle Ann Dodds)
- (optional) digital camera and printer

Helpful Hint

Be sure to have extra wheeled toys available in case someone forgets to bring a toy from home.

Be Safe

Examine the toys brought from home to ensure safety. For example, if a pair of roller skates is brought to school, you will need to set some guidelines regarding when the child may wear the skates and where such activity will take place. Large wagons or similar toys will also require special safety rules.

Getting Ready

- Send letters home prior to Wheel Day.
- On separate index cards, draw or attach photographs of wheeled toys having more or less than four wheels. Since most toys from home will have four wheels, these cards may be needed to provide variety while graphing in step 2. Write the appropriate number of wheels next to each picture.
- Prepare a class graph as shown at right.
- Remove the wheels from a toy car.
- Prepare a wheel chart as shown at right.
- If a slide is not available, set up a ramp either inside or outside.

Spotlight Vocabulary

- move   • friction
- motion words (such as roll and spin)
- force words (such as lift, push, and pull)
- comparison words (such as most, least, and same)
- speed words (such as slow and fast)
- texture words (such as smooth, bumpy, and rough)

Example of class graph on wall

Example of wheel chart on wall

Begin

1. Gather the children with their wheeled toys brought from home. Have each child show his or her toy, tell how many wheels it has, and demonstrate how to move the toy. Record the information on an index card. For example, write "John can push a car with four wheels" or "Mary can ride a tricycle with three wheels." Have the children draw pictures of their toys on their cards. Write the appropriate number of wheels next to each picture. (As an alternative, take a digital picture of each child with his or her toy, attach the picture to a card, and write the caption and wheel number as shown at right.)

2. Tell children that they will now make a graph. Have each child attach their card to a class graph according to the number of wheels. Be sure children understand that the first card in each category should be placed at the bottom of the graph. Subsequent pictures are placed directly above the first pictures to build up the graph from bottom to top. Also ask the children to help attach the pictures you prepared in Getting Ready. (These pictures will offer variety to the results.)

Let's Sing

Rolling Wheels
(sung to the tune of Twinkle, Twinkle Little Star)

Rolling wheels can help things move

Rolling wheels can help things move

Car and trucks and buses, too

Tractors, trains, and airplanes, too

Rolling wheels can help things move

Rolling wheels can help things move

Rolling wheels can help things move

Rolling wheels can help things move

Wagons, bikes, and wheelchairs, too

Skateboards, carts, and strollers, too

Rolling wheels can help things move

Rolling wheels can help things move

3. Point out that a graph is like a picture that tells you something. Ask questions to analyze the data.

Questions to guide the analysis:

> *Most people brought toys with how many wheels? How can you tell?*

> *How many wheels did the fewest people bring? How can you tell?*

Seen and heard:

Children said, "Four wheels is the most," "That part [of the graph] is higher," and "That part is little."

Continue

4. Push a box of blocks across the floor and tell the class that you need to move these blocks to the Block Center. Try pushing the box, but say it is too hard. Ask the class if there is an easier way to move the blocks. (A wagon should be located in close proximity to provide a visual clue.) Hopefully, the children will see the wagon and remember from **Awareness 3: How Can We Move These Books?** that a wagon can help move things. Once the children suggest putting the box of blocks in the wagon, do it. Tell the class that using a wagon with wheels is much easier.

5. Show the class a car with its wheels detached. Let a child try pushing the car across the floor. Then give the child a car with wheels (or put the wheels back on the car) and have him or her push the car with wheels across the floor. Ask which car is easier to move. Point out that wheels help the car move more easily.

6. Ask the children to name things that have wheels. Write each object on a blank index card. Have the children illustrate the cards. Attach a word card to each of the spokes on a paper wheel.

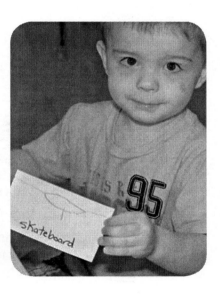

7. Repeat steps 7–10 of **Exploration 3: Ball Day** with the wheeled toys. Be sure the children have opportunities to roll the wheeled toys on different surfaces and at different places in the school.

What to Look For

Look for children to understand that wheels turn and make moving objects easier.

Have More Fun

- ❑ Invite a custodian or delivery person to the classroom to discuss and demonstrate how he or she uses a two-wheeled dolly to move large or heavy objects.

- ❑ Let children ride tricycles, wagons, and other child-sized toys. Be sure the children wear safety helmets.

- ❑ Provide dump trucks and cargo (such as blocks or large beads) for free play. Have the children move the cargo from one area of the room to another area.

- ❑ Use sidewalk chalk on the blacktop to draw city streets. Children can move toy cars and trucks around the city.

- ❑ Have children explore a water wheel at the water table by pouring water over the wheel to make it spin.

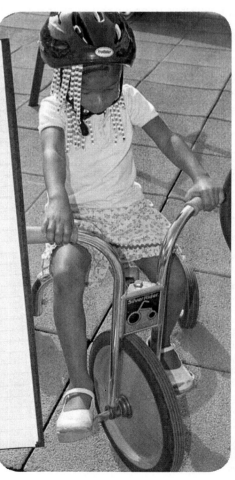

big science
for little hands

Dear Parents:

As part of our science explorations, we are studying objects and how we can make them move. We've already looked at different kinds of objects in our classroom, but now we would like to have a Wheel Day to learn more.

Please join your child in a search for wheeled objects at home. There are many kinds of wheeled objects. Hunt carefully and collect them to examine and compare. Once you have finished hunting for the objects, encourage your child to observe the objects and tell you something about what he or she observes. You might want to assist in this observation by asking several questions: What does this object look like? How many wheels does this object have? What can this object be used for? How are the wheeled objects the same? How are they different?

Have your child choose one favorite wheeled object to bring to school. Put your child's name on the object so it won't get lost.

We will be sharing our wheeled objects in class on Wheel Day. Please help your child to remember to bring his or her wheeled object to school on _____. Thank you for your help. Have fun!

Sincerely,

Exploration 6:
Moving Fun on the Playground

Children discover that they move in different ways on the various pieces of playground equipment.

Duration

1 large group session

Purpose

- use senses to explore real-life movement on the playground
- use good manners, sharing, and safety skills on the playground
- use opposite words (such as up/down, go/stop, and on/off) correctly
- graph results after asking children to pick their favorite playground equipment
- describe playground motions through words and drawings

What You Need

- index cards
- yarn or string
- poster board or large piece of paper
- bulletin board or wall space
- playground equipment (such as slide, seesaw, merry-go-round, and swing) or alternative objects
- ☞ *If one or more of the playground equipment types is not available, try to find toy versions or make representative equipment using craft materials or toy building sets. (See models of swings in **Exploration 1: Push or Pull**)*
- (optional) digital camera and printer
- paper and drawing materials
- (optional) carpet squares, graphing mat, or masking tape

Be Safe

Be sure children follow normal playground safety rules.

Helpful Hint

Every playground has different equipment. Adjust this activity to fit the kind of playground equipment at your school.

Getting Ready

- Designate an area for the "people graph" to be created in step 6. Decide what method will be easiest to help children stand in rows. For example, you can have each child stand on a floor tile, carpet square, graphing mat square, or masking tape line as shown below.

Example of "people graph" on floor

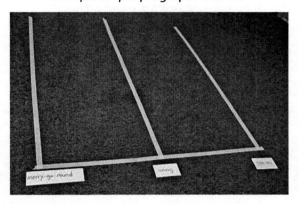

- Use index cards and yarn or string to prepare a class graph on the wall or floor as shown at right. (Children will place their pictures on the graph.)
- Label a bulletin board or wall with the words "Moving Fun on the Playground" as shown at right.
- If you have a digital camera and printer, after step 3 print the photos you took on the playground so each child has two copies of his or her photo for steps 6–8.

Spotlight Vocabulary

- playground
- slide
- swing
- seesaw
- merry-go-round
- opposite words (such as up/down, go/stop, and on/off)
- motion words (such as swing, slide, and spin)
- force words (such as lift, push, and pull)
- speed words (such as slow and fast)

Example of class graph on wall

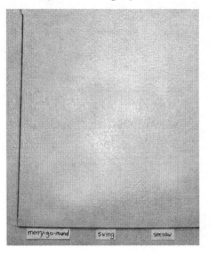

Begin

1. Before going to the playground, tell the children that they should be thinking about how they move on the different playground equipment. Ask the children to think about their favorite part of the playground.

   Questions to guide the inquiry process:
   > *What part of the playground is your favorite?*
   > *How many people like to go down the slide?*
   > *How many people like to go around on the merry-go-round?*
   > *How many people like to swing on the swing?*
   > *How many people like to go up and down on the seesaw?*

2. Take the children to the playground. After 10 minutes of free play, call all the children together and tell them that you would like to take their pictures at their favorite playground area. Tell the children that you will count to three and then they are to walk to their favorite place to play on the playground. Give them the choices of slide, swing, merry-go-round, and seesaw. (Adjust the places according to which equipment is available in your playground.)

3. Count to three and have the children walk to their favorite place to play on the playground. Take each child's picture while he or she is playing on the favorite playground equipment. The pictures will be used in steps 6–8. As an alternative to taking pictures, write each child's name and favorite playground equipment on an index card. Prepare two index cards per child.

4. Once inside, play the opposite game with the children using playground equipment. For example, say to the children, "I climb up on the slide, then I go _____." Point to one of the children to fill in the blank. Then say, "I go up on the swing, then I go _____." Also say, "I go up on the seesaw, then I go _____." Continue the opposite game for several other examples.

5. Give each child a piece of paper and markers or crayons. Tell the children to draw pictures of themselves playing on the playground. Tell them to include all the places that they like to play. Display the pictures in the classroom.

Continue

6. Have each child hold the picture you took of him or her on the playground. Have all the slide people stand in one row in the "people graph" area of the floor that you selected in Getting Ready. Then have the merry-go-round people get in another row. Next have the seesaw people get in a third row and lastly have the swing people get in a fourth row. After the graph is formed, ask regular graphing questions.

Questions to guide the inquiry process:
> *Which place on the playground is the most favorite?…least favorite?*
> *How many people picked the slide as their favorite?*
> *How many people picked the seesaw as their favorite?*

7. Have the children place their pictures in the appropriate columns on a class graph (prepared in Getting Ready). Review the results again if some children had trouble interpreting the "people graph."

8. Give each child another copy of his or her playground picture to glue to the top of a piece of paper. Write the following caption under the picture as each child fills in the blanks: "I can _____ when I play on the _____." Assemble the pages into a class book.

9. Write the captions of the class book pages on index cards and post the cards on a bulletin board or poster under the title "Moving Fun on the Playground" as shown at left. Add pictures if you want. The class graph, book, and bulletin board will be used in **Application 2: Design Some Fun**.

What to Look For

Encourage the children to look at the playground equipment in a scientific way. Model words during discussions that refer to the motions that the children experience on the playground.

Exploration 7:
Sliding, Sliding, Down and Down

Children explore how different objects slide down different ramp surfaces.

Duration

1 large group session

Purpose

- observe and experiment with different objects going down ramps made from different materials
- communicate observations about object movement down the ramps
- compare ramps and determine which ramp objects go down the fastest
- use good manners and sharing skills

What You Need

- about 4–5 rectangle-shaped trays (such as cookie sheets, cafeteria trays, or shallow baking pans) that are the same size and shape
- various materials to lay over the trays (such as bubble wrap, towel, waxed paper, sandpaper, or other materials with interesting textures)

☞ *Be sure to choose smooth and rough materials.*

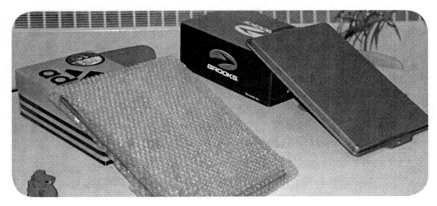

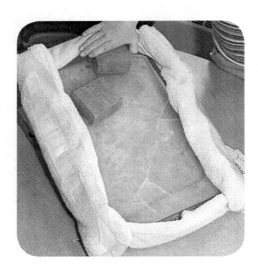

- masking tape
- freezer
- books, blocks, or boxes to prop up ramps
- small blocks to slide down ramps
- playground slide
- (optional) book about sledding, such as *The Wild Toboggan Ride* (by Suzan Reid and Eugenie Fernandez)

Getting Ready

- At least one day before doing the activity, fill a tray with water and place on a level shelf in the freezer to make an ice ramp. (You may want to make more than one ice ramp so you'll have replacements when the first ice ramp starts melting.) Before class, wrap and tape a towel around the metal tray as shown at left so only the ice is exposed.

- Prepare other tray ramps by wrapping various materials around the backs of the trays and taping in place as shown below. Leave one tray as is.

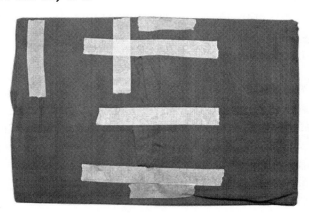

- Experiment with the blocks and ramps to decide how high to make the ramps. All ramps need to be set at the same height.

Spotlight Vocabulary

- surface
- height
- ice
- ramp
- gravity
- melt
- texture words (such as smooth, bumpy, and rough)
- speed words (such as slow, slowest, fast, and fastest)
- motion words (such as slide and roll)

Begin

1. Gather the children around the ramps prepared in Getting Ready. Review what the class has discovered with ramps, wheels, balls, and other objects. Tell the children that now the class will explore different ramp surfaces.

2. Use a block to model how to use the ramps. Emphasize that objects should be placed at the top of the ramps and let go. (Reinforce that objects should not be pushed.) Tell the children that gravity is pulling the block down the ramp. Children should watch how the block slides down the ramp.

3. Show and discuss the different ramp surfaces. Point out that all the ramps are at the same height. Ask children to predict which surfaces the block will move down the fastest and the slowest.

Sci-Lit Connection

You can begin this activity by reading the class a book about sledding, such as *The Wild Toboggan Ride* (by Suzan Reid and Eugenie Fernandez).

4. Have each child use one block to try each ramp. Emphasize that the children need to take turns when exploring the ramps. Encourage children to share their observations when comparing how fast their blocks slide down the various ramps.

5. Gather the class to discuss their observations.

Questions to guide the comparing process:

> *Which ramp was the fastest?…the slowest?*
> *Which ramp would be the most fun to go down?*
> *What is happening to the ice ramp as time goes on? Why is the ice ramp melting?*
> *Why don't we make playground slides out of ice?*

Seen and heard:

Children said, "The ice slides faster," "Wax paper is fast," and "The furry thing is slow."

Continue

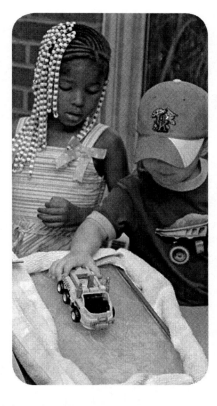

6. Tell children to gather objects around the room to try on the ramps. Encourage children to share their observations when watching their objects go down the various ramps. Point out that some objects roll rather than slide down the ramps.

7. Take the collection of objects to the playground and try each object on the playground slide.

What to Look For

Look to ensure that the children are letting go of the objects at the top of the ramps rather than pushing. Children should notice a difference between the ramps and how the objects travel down the ramps.

Have More Fun

☐ In warm weather, lay out a large piece of plastic on the grass. Wet the plastic with water and add a small amount of child-safe safe soap or bubble bath. Child can wear swimsuits and have fun sliding on the plastic.

Exploration 8:
Going, Going, Up and Down

Children use a balance and playground seesaw to explore up and down motion.

Duration

1 large group session and independent exploration

Purpose

- observe up and down motion
- discover how a balance works to compare weights
- observe cause and effect
- predict and communicate which objects are heavier and which are lighter than a toy animal
- group objects based on how their weights compare to the weight of a toy animal
- apply experiences with a balance when exploring a playground seesaw

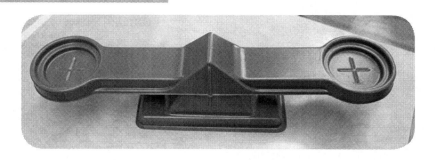

What You Need

- index cards
- primary or bucket balance
- one or more toy animals
- 🍎 *If you begin the activity by reading a story about an animal on a seesaw, try to choose that type of toy animal.*
- objects that weigh the same, more, and less than the toy animal
- designated sorting areas made with yarn, masking tape, hula-hoops, or small rugs (prepared in Getting Ready)
- playground seesaw
- (optional) book about seesaws, such as *Just a Little Bit* (by Ann Tompert)

Be Safe

Be sure children follow normal playground safety rules.

Helpful Hint

The term "weight" is used in this activity since the term "mass" is outside the realm of young children's understanding. (See **Part 8: All About Motion** for further explanation.)

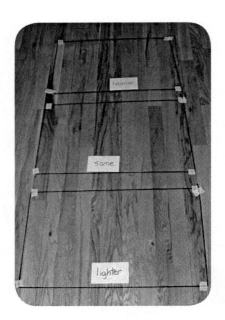

Getting Ready

- Set up designated sorting areas by either marking out areas of about 3 feet × 3 feet with yarn or tape or laying out objects (such as hula-hoops or rugs). Write or draw on index cards to label the areas "heavier," "same," and "lighter" as shown at left.

Spotlight Vocabulary

- balance (the equipment)
- gravity • seesaw
- direction words (such as up and down)
- comparison words (such as heavier/lighter and bigger/smaller)

Sci-Lit Connection

You can begin this activity by reading the class a book about seesaws, such as *Just a Little Bit* (by Ann Tompert).

Begin

1. Place a toy animal on one side of a balance. Point out that gravity made that side of the balance go down. Ask the class what they think can be put on the other side of the balance so that the animal will go up.

   ### Question to guide the inquiry process:
   > *What object or group of objects will be heavier than the animal?*

2. Ask the children to gather objects from the classroom that might make the animal go up. As a class, try different objects and different combinations of objects. Give children a chance to gather and try additional objects. If you have different kinds or sizes of toy animals, you can also have the children determine which of the toy animals is the heaviest.

Seen and heard:
Children said, "That side goes down," "It's the same now," and "It's like a teeter totter."

3. Leave these materials in the Math or Sensory Center for free exploration.

Continue

4. Show children the collection that they will sort into objects that are heavier than the toy animal, objects that are lighter than the animal, and objects that are the same weight as the animal (objects that make the balance "balance").

5. Place the animal on the balance. Hold up an object and ask children to predict if it is heavier, lighter, or weighs the same as the animal. Try it. Place the object in the appropriate sorting area.

6. Repeat step 5 with the rest of the collection.

Helpful Hint

Although you have already assembled a collection of objects, add some objects tested in step 2 to the step 4 collection so children can experience satisfaction in making correct predictions during step 5.

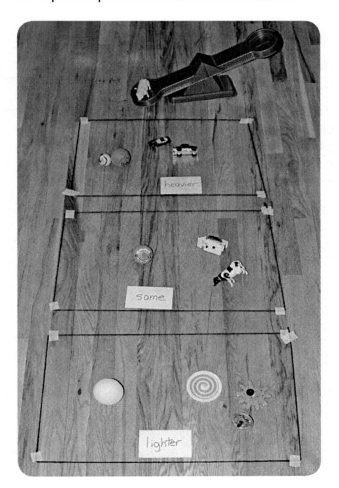

7. Go to the playground to explore a real seesaw.

What to Look For

Look for an understanding of the balance as children try to make the toy animal go up. Children should understand which side of the balance holds more weight as they sort objects into heavier, lighter, and the same weight as the toy animal. The children should be able to relate the outside experience on the seesaw with their experiences with the balance.

Stop and Reflect

Using the class charts from previous activities for reference, review with the children what they have discovered so far about moving objects. Ask the children to share additional discoveries. You may wish to add ideas to the same charts or start a new chart summarizing their discoveries so far.

Guide the reflection process by asking

- What do you know about moving objects now?
- What is interesting about moving objects?
- What else would you like to know about moving objects?
- How could we find out more?

Tell the children that they will be finding out more about moving objects as scientists would do—by doing experiments with different moving objects and the materials that make them. To include the children in the inquiry process, ask the class what they would like to know about moving objects and how they could find answers. Children may surprise you with great ideas that are different than your plans. You may be able to incorporate their ideas into activities during the next phase of the learning cycle, the inquiry phase. There may be some questions that can't be answered easily—or sometimes not at all. That's okay. Scientists don't know everything and neither do we. On the other hand, we might be able to find out more in the future!

What to look for

All children can contribute something to explain what they have discovered during the unit so far. Some may need to refer to materials or samples of their work for ideas.

Part 3: Inquiry

What is the inquiry phase?

The inquiry phase of the learning cycle enables children to deepen and refine their understanding.

During inquiry, children

- examine,

- investigate,

- propose explanations,

- compare own thinking with that of others,

- generalize, and

- relate to prior learning.

The teacher's role is to

- help children refine understanding,

- ask more focused questions,

- provide information when requested, and

- help children make connections between prior experiences and their current investigations.

Inquiry 1:

Ramp It Up

Children practice predicting while a toy car is repeatedly released down a ramp. The class gathers more information when the ramp incline is increased.

Duration

1 large group session

Purpose

- practice predicting and measuring results
- share observations and discuss class results
- observe that a toy car rolls down a ramp
- observe how changes in ramp heights affect the movement of a toy car

What You Need

- permanent marker
- removable pointers such as Post-it® flags or craft sticks
- ramp

☞ *You can prop up stiff cardboard or a wooden board with books, blocks, or boxes. For this activity you must use same-sized objects to support the ramp.*

- about 4–6 yardsticks or metersticks
- object showing units of measure that children can understand and count (such as tile floor squares, masking tape with lines drawn at equal distances, checkered tablecloth with large squares, graphing mat with squares, or Wipe-Off® Graphing Grid)
- masking tape
- toy car

☞ *Select a car that follows a relatively straight path.*

- poster board or large piece of paper
- (optional) book about a vehicle rolling down a hill, such as *Sputter, Sputter, Sput!* (by Babs Bell)

Getting Ready

- Write letters on the pointers as shown so children can identify their own pointer. Prepare one pointer for each child.

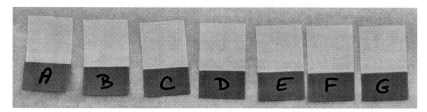

- Set up the ramp. Tape yardsticks or metersticks on both sides of the lane to help the car go straight. Arrange materials so that the units of measure start at the base of the ramp and extend along the floor. Make sure the toy car will not roll over anything that will impede movement.

- Use same-sized objects to prop up the ramp. Test and select ramp heights that allow the toy car to travel within measurable distances at three different heights. Finish by setting the ramp in its lowest position.

- Prepare a class chart as shown at right. In the Ramp Height column, enter the number of objects used to support the ramp at the three different heights. (For example, one box, two boxes, and three boxes.)

Example of class chart

Ramp Height	Distance		

Spotlight Vocabulary

- gravity
- ramp
- stop
- roll
- direction words (such as up and down)
- speed words (such as slow, slower, fast, and faster)
- comparison words (such as higher/lower and heavier/lighter)

Begin

1. With the ramp set at its lowest position, review with the class how to use a ramp. Demonstrate how to place the toy car at the top of the ramp and then let go without pushing. Ask children to observe what happens. Tell the children that gravity is pulling the object down the ramp so the car does not need a push.

Questions to guide the observing process:

> *What happens to the car on the ramp?*
> *Does the car need a push? Why not?*

Sci-Lit Connection

You can begin this activity by reading the class a book about a vehicle rolling down a hill, such as *Sputter, Sputter, Sput!* (by Babs Bell).

2. Make a line at the top of the ramp and tell the class that you will begin the car at this line every time it is let go. Release the car from the line, letting it roll down the ramp and onto the floor until it stops rolling. Point out where the car stops and repeat the process several more times.

3. Ask each child to place a pointer where he or she thinks the car will stop after rolling down the ramp again. Tell children that they are making a prediction. Explain that a prediction is a guess that is based on things they already know or have seen before.

4. Release the car from the line on the ramp and place a piece of tape at the spot where the car stops. Label the tape with the number of objects used to support the ramp. Ask which of the class pointers are the closest to the real stopping point and which pointers are the farthest away. Point out (if this is the case) that the car went past some pointers and didn't get as far as other pointers. Show the children how to count the units along the pathway and record the data on the class chart.

5. Repeat steps 3 and 4 two more times. Notice if the children are getting better at predicting the results.

   Questions to guide the predicting process:
   > *What do you notice about where the car stops each time?*
   > *What is important to remember?*

   Seen and heard:
   > *Children said, "The car stops right here," "It stopped on the nine again," and "It stopped by mine!"*

A prediction is a guess that is based on things already known or previously seen.

Continue

6. Ask the children what can be done to make the car go farther. Guide the children to the idea of raising the ramp to increase the incline. Raise the ramp to the next height you selected in Getting Ready. Release the car from the line, letting it roll down the ramp and onto the floor until it stops rolling. Point out where the car stops and repeat the process several more times.

7. Repeat steps 3–5 with the second ramp height.

8. Raise the ramp to the third ramp height you selected in Getting Ready and release the car down the ramp several times. Repeat steps 3–5 with the third ramp height.

9. Ask the class to look at the class chart and discuss the results. Children should notice that the higher the ramp, the farther the car goes.

Children watch to see which pointers are the closest to the car's stopping point.

What to Look For

Prediction skills may improve as children gain more experience during the activity. Look for the understanding that the higher the ramp, the faster and farther the car goes.

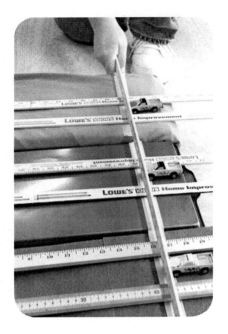

Inquiry 2:
Rough Road Ahead

Children continue their investigations of ramps by trying ramps made from different materials.

Duration

1 large group session

Purpose

- observe how different ramp surfaces affect the movement of a toy car
- observe that toy cars roll down ramps
- practice predicting and measuring results
- share observations and discuss class results

What You Need

- permanent marker
- 3 different colors of removable pointers (such as Post-it® flags or craft sticks)
- colored stickers matching the colors of the pointers
- 3 identical toy cars
- ☞ *Select cars that follow a relatively straight path.*
- 3 ramps covered with assorted textures as in **Exploration 7: Sliding, Sliding, Down and Down**
- ☞ *Be sure to include one smooth surface and two rougher surfaces (such as sandpaper and cloth). Rather than three separate ramps, you could also use the alternative ramp setup as shown at left.*
- 3 or more same-sized books, boxes, or large blocks
- masking tape
- 6–12 yardsticks or metersticks
- object showing units of measure that children can understand and count (such as tile floor squares, masking tape with lines drawn at equal distances, checkered tablecloth with large squares, graphing mat with squares, or Wipe-Off® Graphing Grid)
- poster board or large piece of paper

An alternative to three ramps is a single piece of foam board covered with assorted textures.

Getting Ready

- Each child will get one pointer of each color to predict travel distances. Write letters on the pointers as shown at right so each child will be assigned the same letter for each pointer color. (For example, Wyatt will get blue, yellow, and red pointers marked with the letter B.)

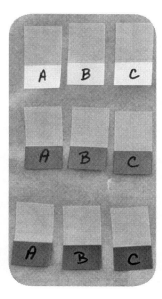

- Assign each car a color that matches one of the pointer colors the children will use when predicting travel distances. Mark the tops of the cars with colored stickers that correspond to the pointer colors. You will use additional stickers of the same colors to mark the floor where the cars stop.

- Set up the three ramps side-by-side. Tape yardsticks or metersticks on both sides of each lane to help the cars go straight as shown at right. Arrange the materials so that the units of measure start at the base of the ramps and extend along the floor. Make sure the toy cars will not roll over anything that will impede movement.

- Test and select one ramp height that allows the toy cars to travel within measurable distances. All ramps should be set at the same height.

- Prepare a class chart as shown at right. In the Ramp column, fill in the textures of the ramps to be tested.

Spotlight Vocabulary

- gravity
- ramp
- stop
- roll
- direction words (such as up and down)
- speed words (such as slow, slower, fast, and faster)
- comparison words (such as higher/lower and heavier/lighter)
- texture words (such as smooth, bumpy, and rough)

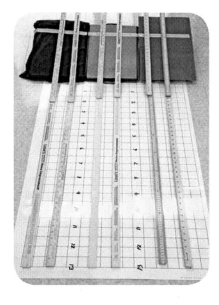

Example of class chart

Ramp	Distance		

Begin

1. Review with the class how to use a ramp. Demonstrate how to place a toy car at the top of the ramp and then let go without pushing. Tell the children that gravity is pulling the object down the ramp so the car does not need a push.

2. Make a line at the top of the ramps and tell the class that you will begin the cars at the line every time they are let go. Use a yardstick to hold all the cars at the starting line. Lift the yardstick to release the cars from the line at the same time. Let the cars roll down the ramp and onto the floor until they stop rolling. Discuss where the cars stop and repeat the process several more times.

3. Ask each child to place a pointer where he or she predicts each of the cars will stop after rolling down the ramps again. Remind children to use the correct pointers by matching the color of the pointer to the color of the sticker on the car.

4. Lift the yardstick to release the cars down the ramp. Place an appropriately colored sticker where each car stops. Ask which of the children's pointers are the closest to the real stopping points and which pointers are the farthest away. Point out (if this is the case) that cars went past some pointers and didn't get as far as other pointers. Show the children how to count the units along the pathway and record the data on the class chart.

5. Repeat steps 3 and 4 two more times. Notice if the children are getting better at predicting the results.

Continue

6. Ask the class to look at the class chart and compare the results. Children should notice that the cars traveling down the rougher ramps do not go as far as the car traveling down the smooth ramp. Point out that friction causes the cars to slow down and stop. There are different amounts of friction on the three ramp surfaces so the cars move differently.

Example of class chart showing data

Ramp	Distance		
cloth	7	7	4
metal	13	13	13
sandpaper	10	11	9

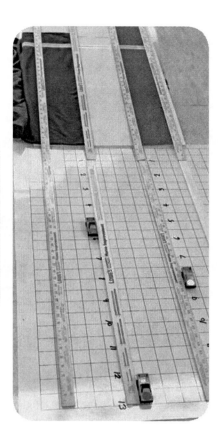

Questions to guide the observing and comparing processes:

> *What is different about the ramps?*
> *How do the cars move differently?*
> *Which car goes the farthest? Why?*
> *Why do all the cars slow down and stop?*

Seen and heard:

> *Children said, "This feels rough," "That ramp is bumpy," and "That car goes super fast."*

What to Look For

Look for children to make conclusions and comparisons about the car's performance on different ramp surfaces. For example, they may conclude that cars traveling down rougher ramps do not go as far. Some children may be able to conclude that the car stops sooner on those ramp surfaces that create more friction.

Have More Fun

☐ Try repeating the procedure with the three ramps at three different heights. Prior to class, test and select ramp heights that allow all of the cars on all of the ramps to travel within measurable distances at three different ramps heights. During class, state that you wonder how far the cars will travel when the ramps are at the three different heights you have selected. Do steps 3–5 of the procedure. Ask the class to look at the class chart and discuss the results.

Inquiry 3:
Up and Down Seesaw

Children use balances to model how a seesaw works.

Duration

1 large group session and independent exploration

Purpose

- observe that putting an object on one side of a balance or seesaw makes that side go down
- match the weights of objects to counters serving as weights
- watch the balance to see when the weights on the two sides of the balance match
- count the number of counters that made the balance level
- compare the weights of various objects
- practice predicting and measuring results
- learn that science involves trial and error

What You Need

- poster board or large piece of paper
- primary or bucket balances
- set of same-sized counters (such as plastic counting bears or centimeter/gram cubes)
- collection of stuffed animals and dolls that fit on the balance
- ⓕ *Make sure each toy weighs at least one counter but no more than about 20 counters.*

Be Safe

Remind children not to put small objects in their mouths.

Getting Ready

Prepare a class chart as shown at right.

Example of class chart

Name	Toy	Number of Bears

Spotlight Vocabulary
- balance
- objects
- weigh/weight
- counters
- comparison words (such as more/less and heavy/light)

Begin

1. Demonstrate how to use a balance by first placing a toy from the collection on one side of the balance. Point out that gravity made that side of the balance go down. Use counters to determine the weight (number of counters) of the toy. Enter the weight on the first line of the class chart. Have each child pick another toy from the collection. Tell the children that you wonder how much their toys weigh.

2. Have children work in pairs so they can help each other. Ask each child to weigh his or her toy by putting the toy on one side and enough counters on the other side to make the balance level. Then, children should count the number of counters they used and record the results on the class chart. (Younger children may need help recording their results.)

> ### Helpful Hint
> If children are not familiar with balances, giving them free exploration time prior to this activity will help the children focus better in step 2.

Continue

3. Gather the class together around the class chart. Ask each child to explain what they found out, then ask the class to compare and discuss results.

4. Select two children having toys with significantly different weights. Point out how many counters each of the toys weighs based on the class chart results. Ask the class to predict what would happen to the balance if the toys were put on opposite sides of the balance. Try it to confirm the answer.

   ### Question to guide the predicting process:
   > *His toy weighs three bears and her toy weighs nine bears. If I put his toy on one side of the balance, what will happen to the balance when I put her toy on the other side?*

   ### Seen and heard:
   Children said, "I don't know" and "Hers will go down."

5. Repeat step 4 until children are comfortable with using the class chart to predict results.

6. Tell the children to pretend the balance is a seesaw. Select two children having toys with significantly different weights. Have the children put their toys on opposite sides of the balance. Ask the class what can be done to make the "seesaw" balance. Try the children's suggestions. Be sure to try adding objects to the lighter side of the balance, such as counters, someone else's toy, and a combination of both counters and toys.

Questions to guide the inquiry:
> *How can we make the seesaw balance?*
> *What would happen if we put things on this side?*

Children cheer as the two sides balance.

7. Make the balances and toys available for free exploration.

What to Look For

Look for an understanding of the balance as children determine the weights of their toys. Children should understand which side of the balance holds more weight as they add and remove counters during the weighing process. Later as children compare toys and make predictions about which side of the balance will go down, look for an understanding of how to analyze the results on the class chart.

Stop and Reflect

Set up a display of the children's recorded observations. In small groups, meet with the children to view and discuss the display. Record their ideas and add them to the display for others to see. Read their ideas aloud to the class.

Guide the discussion process by asking

- What do you think about your own work?
- What do you notice about ramps by looking at the group's work?
- What do you want to remember about balances?
- What was something new that you learned by doing these activities?
- What is important to remember about ramps?

Part 4:
Advanced Inquiry

How are advanced inquiry activities different?

Advanced inquiry activities are provided for children who are ready to experiment further. The first advanced inquiry activity expands the use of ramps as children are challenged to make a car go over a hill and around a loop without touching the car. The second activity challenges children to design a ramp amusement ride. The third activity allows children to plan and test their own procedures based on what they wonder about motion.

Advanced Inquiry 1:
Hill and Loop Challenges

Children are challenged to get a toy car up and over a hill without pushing the car. Then, children apply what they learn about the hill challenge to get a car around a loop.

Duration

1 large group session and independent exploration

Purpose

- apply what was learned about ramps to solve two challenges
- learn how to solve a challenge based on trial and error
- work like scientists during the redesign process by thinking logically and trying over and over

What You Need

- plastic track at least 8 feet long
- ⑤ *Connect sections of plastic race car track (such as Darda® or Hot Wheels®) together to make one long track.*
- toy car that fits on the track
- objects to prop up the track (such as wooden board, stiff cardboard, boxes, blocks, or books)
- track loop

Getting Ready

- Set up the hilled track as shown at left by placing objects under the track to make a hill. Mark a line on one end of the track to designate the starting line. Make sure a toy car that is pushed towards the hill will make it over. Also test to determine if the car will go over the hill when one, two, and more objects are placed under the starting line to make ramps of different inclines. Ideally the car should not go over when one object is used to prop up the ramp, but should go over when more objects are used to prop up the ramp.

starting line   plastic track

hill

- Set up the looped track as shown at right. Test to determine if a car will go around the loop when one, two, and more objects are placed under the starting line to make ramps of different inclines. Ideally the car should not go around the loop when one object is used to prop up the track, but should go around when more objects are used to prop up the track.

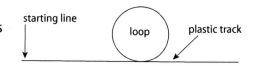

Spotlight Vocabulary
- challenge
- push
- over
- speed words (such as slow and fast)

Begin

1. Show children the hill and the starting line. Ask the class how to get a car over the hill. After hearing suggestions, let a child try pushing and releasing the car towards the hill. If the car doesn't make it, have the child try pushing the car harder.

2. Now tell the children that you wonder if there is a way to get the car to go over the hill without pushing it. Try placing the car at the line and letting go. When the car doesn't move, ask children what you should do. Demonstrate that telling the car to move doesn't work. If the class has already done **Inquiry 1: Ramp It Up** or **Inquiry 2: Rough Road Ahead**, ask children to think about what they did in those activities to make the car move. Guide the children to suggest making a ramp to raise the starting line.

3. Put one object under the starting line to create a ramp. (Also placing a board or stiff cardboard under the ramp will help keep the track rigid.) Ask a child to let the car go at the starting line. When the car doesn't go over the hill, ask the children what should be done. Point out that only one thing at a time should be changed during the redesign process so that you'll know what change causes the car to go over the hill. (This concept models how experimenting scientists change one variable at a time.) Guide the children to suggest adding another object under the starting line.

4. Continue to add objects, one at a time, under the starting line until the car makes it over the hill.

Continue

Helpful Hint

If needed, guide the children to suggest adding one or more objects under the starting line to make a ramp. If the car still doesn't go around the loop, try making the ramp higher.

5. Show children the loop and the starting line. Tell the children that you wonder if there is a way to get the car around the loop without pushing it. Ask the children to work together and try different things until the car makes it around the loop. Emphasize that the children should change one thing at a time during the redesign process so they'll know what change causes the car to go around the loop. Allow children to try their ideas until they're successful.

Question to guide the design process:

> *What can we do to get the car around the loop without pushing it?*

Seen and heard:

Children said, "Make it higher," "Boxes will totally work," and "One more!"

6. If you have room, leave the hill and loop setups available for free exploration.

What to Look For

Children should understand that the car will not move by itself. Look for children to understand that raising the ramp makes the car go faster. When the ramp is raised high enough to make the car go fast enough, the car makes it over the hill and around the loop.

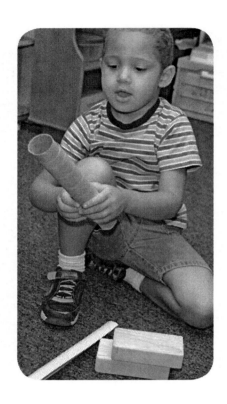

Advanced Inquiry 2:
Design a Fun Ramp Ride

Children are challenged to design a ride that includes a ramp to start the motion.

Duration
1 large group session

Purpose
- use knowledge of ramps to design a ramp ride
- communicate and work cooperatively to design a ride
- describe and demonstrate the design to the class

What You Need
- empty cardboard tubes from paper towels and wrapping paper
- scissors
- ramp materials (such as cardboard, foam board, and lightweight wood)
- masking tape, string, and rubber bands
- small vehicles and balls
- paper and drawing materials
- (optional) digital camera and printer
- (optional) marble rolling toy as shown at left

Be Safe
Remind children not to put small objects in their mouths.

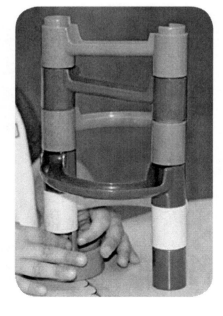

Getting Ready
Cut some of the cardboard tubes in half lengthwise as shown at right to make channels for the vehicles and balls.

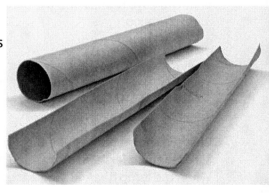

Spotlight Vocabulary
- design
- roll
- gravity
- ramp
- ride

Begin

1. Ask the children to draw a design for the greatest ramp ever made. Ask them if they ever rode on an amusement park ride that had a ramp.

2. Give the children tubes, ramps, vehicles, and balls. Demonstrate how the vehicles and balls can go through the tubes and channels you prepared in Getting Ready. Remind children that gravity is pulling the objects down.

3. Ask children to experiment with the vehicles and balls rolling through the tubes and down the ramps. Walk around and ask children to demonstrate what they have discovered.

    Questions to guide the discovery process:
    > What have you discovered about your ramp?
    > How do the tubes and channels help the ball move?

Continue

4. Ask children to work in pairs to design rides with the materials. Provide tape, string, and rubber bands so children can connect things together in different ways. Guide children to realize that ramps can get the rides started.

5. When children are done designing, ask each group to demonstrate to the class how their ride works. Make sure children use motion words in their descriptions.

6. Take a photo of each design or have children draw pictures. Add a sentence to summarize the design. Display the pictures and make materials available so others can build the designs.

7. If available, have children explore with a marble rolling toy.

What to Look For

Look for children to understand that they can use tubes and channels to change, direct, and control the movement of rolling objects. Watch for good cooperation skills with each pair of children.

Advanced Inquiry 3:
I Wonder...

Children participate in discovery activities about motion.

Duration
2 large group sessions and 1 small group session

Purpose
- experience the process of discovery by asking questions, planning and doing investigations, and recording results
- communicate results to the class

What You Need
- poster board or large piece of paper
- class charts and children's work from previous activities
- materials determined by the children
- I Wonder Data Sheet (provided at the end of this activity)

Getting Ready
- Prepare a We Wonder class chart as shown below.
- Make copies of the I Wonder Data Sheet. You may want to make extras in case some children need to start over.

Spotlight Vocabulary
- investigate
- experiment
- plan
- test
- wonder
- record

Example of class chart

Class Chart

We wonder _____

What We Plan to Do

What We Found Out

Process Skill Power

"What separates true inquiry from play are the processes of observing and questioning, and then developing and following a plan of action."

Jane Bresnick, 2000

"I wonder if a bumpy ball will go down a ramp faster than a regular ball."

1. Ask children to share what they have learned about motion. Show the class charts and work from previous activities. Remind children about all the things they have wondered about and all the things that they've found out. Explain that scientists are always looking for more to learn. Model the inquiry process by making an "I wonder" statement that is easily testable. (See example at left.)

2. Write down your "I wonder" statement on the class chart prepared in Getting Ready. Ask the children specific questions to come up with a plan for testing the "I wonder" statement. (See Helpful Hint at left.) Draw a picture depicting the plan in the "What We Plan to Do" section of the class chart. (See photo below.)

Questions to guide the inquiry:
> *How can we test what we are wondering about?*
> *What things do we need for our test?*

Helpful Hint

Ask the children detailed questions during the planning stage, such as "Which balls should be tested? Should the balls be the same size? How should we make the ramp? How should we measure which ball goes down the ramp faster? Should we let the balls go down the ramp at the same time?"

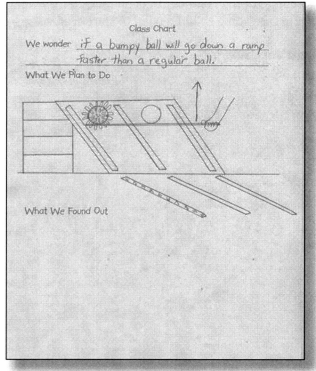

Example of a class plan

3. As a class, conduct the test outlined by the children. With the help of the children, complete the "What We Found Out" section of the class chart.

Continue

4. Working in small groups, ask the children what other things they wonder about motion. It may be helpful to review the previous activities that they did. Describing previous procedures and results may help children think of things they still wonder about.

Helpful Hints

Allow the children to come up with their own plan for testing the "I wonder" statement. The investigation process is much more meaningful to children when they design and implement their own procedures rather than use procedures outlined by the teacher.

During the inquiry process, the teacher should observe, question, and support the efforts of the children. Some redirecting of the children's plans may be necessary. You may also have to assist some children who have a hard time articulating their ideas by helping them find the right words.

5. Ask the children in each small group to come up with one "I wonder" statement that relates to motion. Guide the children to discuss and agree upon one plan for testing their statement. Introduce the term "experiment." Help the group fill out an I Wonder Data Sheet (prepared in Getting Ready) by writing out their "I wonder" statement and then drawing a procedure in the "What I Plan to Do" portion of the data sheet. Older children may fill out their own data sheets.

Questions to guide the inquiry process:
> *What do you wonder about motion?*
> *How can you test your idea?*
> *What do you need to use for your experiment?*

6. Have the children conduct their experiment, and then assist the group as needed in drawing and writing to complete the "What I Found Out" portion of the data sheet.

7. Gather the class together and ask each group of children to show their data sheets and describe their findings.

What to Look For

Becoming comfortable with the inquiry learning process takes lots of time and practice. Some children may have difficulty with some or all of the questioning, planning, testing, and recording steps. Modeling the process and working with children in small groups will help them learn the inquiry process.

I Wonder Data Sheet

Name _____

I wonder _____

_____

What I Plan to Do

What I Found Out

Stop and Reflect

After investigating more about motion, review with children what they have discovered so far. Keep a record of the children's ideas to show the progress of their learning.

Guide the reflection process by asking

- What can you tell people about motion?
- What new things did you discover in your work?
- Were you surprised by anything that happened during your experiment?
- What did you notice?
- What else about motion would you like to know and find out? How could you do that?

What to look for

Children have now had a variety of experiences with motion. They have explored the materials with teacher guidance and then more independently. During reflection, listen for details about their experiences. Some children may focus on the processes they used to explore. Other children may focus on the results and their observations of the experiments themselves.

Encourage children to be descriptive and offer ideas to explain what they have learned. Instill pride in their accomplishments; they have done experiments just like scientists do.

Part 5: Application

What is the application phase?

In the application phase, learners apply their understandings in new settings and situations. The activities in this phase can also serve as assessment tools.

During application, children

- apply what they have learned in new situations,
- represent learning in various ways, and
- formulate new hypotheses and repeat the learning cycle.

The teacher's role is to

- create links for application in the world outside the classroom,
- provide meaningful situations in which children use what they have learned, and
- help children apply learning to new situations.

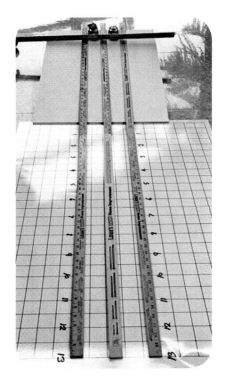

Application 1:
Loaded Question

Children predict and compare how empty and full toy dump trucks travel down a ramp.

Duration
1 large group session

Purpose
- compare travel distances down a ramp for an empty toy dump truck and a full one
- review that toy trucks roll down a ramp
- practice predicting and measuring results
- share observations and discuss class results

What You Need
- permanent marker
- 2 different colors of removable pointers (such as Post-it® flags or craft sticks)
- colored stickers matching the colors of the pointers
- 2 identical toy dump trucks (capable of holding rocks)

☞ *Select trucks that follow a relatively straight path.*

- rocks that fit in the toy dump truck
- ramp

☞ *You can prop up stiff cardboard or a wooden board with books, blocks, or boxes. The ramp should be wide enough so the two toy dump trucks can go down the ramp at the same time.*

- about 10 yardsticks or metersticks
- masking tape
- object showing units of measure that children can understand and count (such as tile floor squares, masking tape with lines drawn at equal distances, checkered tablecloth with large squares, graphing mat with squares, or Wipe-Off® Graphing Grid)
- poster board or large piece of paper
- primary or bucket balance

Getting Ready

- Each child will get one pointer of each color to predict travel distances. Write letters on the pointers so each child will be assigned the same letter for each pointer color. (For example, Breanna will get a blue pointer and a red pointer marked with the letter A.)

- Assign each toy dump truck a color that matches one of the pointer colors the children will use when predicting travel distances. Mark the tops of the trucks with colored stickers that correspond to the pointer colors. (You will use additional stickers of the same colors to mark the floor where the trucks stop.)

- Set up the ramp. Tape yardsticks or metersticks on both sides of the lane to help the car go straight. Arrange materials so that the units of measure start at the base of the ramp and extend along the floor. Make sure the toy car will not roll over anything that will impede movement.

- Test and select a ramp height that allows both empty and full toy dump trucks to travel within measurable distances.

- Prepare a class chart as shown at right. Enter the ramp height you determined was the best for your setup.

Spotlight Vocabulary

- gravity
- ramp
- stop
- roll
- direction words (such as up and down)
- speed words (such as slow, slower, fast, and faster)
- comparison words (such as higher/lower and heavier/lighter)

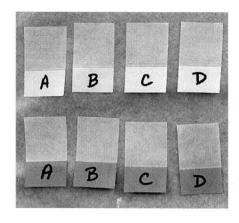

Example of class chart

Ramp Height	Distance Truck Traveled	
	Empty	Full

Begin

1. Ask a volunteer to review how a balance works, then use the balance to show the class that the two toy trucks you selected weigh the same. Next ask the children if a truck full of rocks weighs less, the same, or more than an empty truck. Have a volunteer add rocks to one of the trucks on the balance so the class can observe the results.

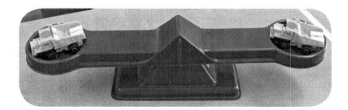

2. Tell the children that you wonder if the truck holding the rocks will travel farther down the ramp than the empty truck. Ask the children to predict what will happen. Guide children as they discuss ways of finding out.

Continue

3. Show children the items you prepared in Getting Ready. Let older children design and conduct the experiments discussed in step 2. Younger children may need more guidance. For example, children can do steps 3–5 of **Inquiry 1: Ramp It Up.** Place both trucks on the line at the top of the ramp and use a yardstick to release both trucks at the same time. Place an appropriately colored sticker where each truck stops.

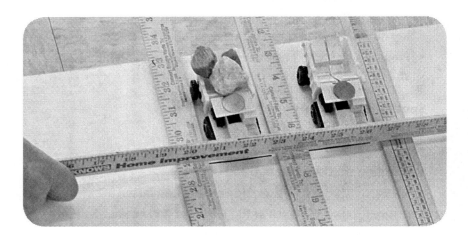

4. Ask the class to look at the class chart and discuss the results. Children should identify which truck went further.

   Questions to guide the discussion:
   > *What did you notice about the travel distances of the two trucks?*
   > *How does changing the weight of the truck make a difference?*

What to Look For

Prediction skills may get better as children gain more experience during the activity. Assess whether the children understand which truck travels further. Most of the time, the full truck will go further than the empty truck. However, if friction is greater between the full truck and the ramp than between the empty truck and the ramp, the full truck will slow down sooner and not travel as far.

Have More Fun

☐ Prior to class, test and select ramp heights that allow both empty and full trucks to travel within measurable distances at three different heights. During class, explain to the children that you wonder how far the empty and full trucks will travel when the ramp is at the three different heights you decided upon prior to class. Point out that all of the objects used to prop up the ramp have to be exactly the same so the results can be compared. Guide the children as they do steps 2–5 of **Inquiry 1: Ramp It Up** with both trucks going down the ramp at the same time. Ask the class to look at the class chart and discuss the results.

Application 2:
Design Some Fun

Children apply the knowledge they have gained about motion to create miniature playgrounds or amusement rides.

Duration

1 large group session

Purpose

- use different materials in different ways to show motion
- communicate and work cooperatively to design and create a miniature playground or amusement ride
- describe and demonstrate his or her design to the class

What You Need

- class graph, book, and bulletin board prepared in **Exploration 6: Moving Fun on the Playground**
- materials to make miniature playground equipment or amusement rides
- ⓕ *Gather materials such as paper tubes, cardboard, plastic cups and bowls, blocks, boxes, pipe cleaners, string, tape, and rubber bands.*
- small objects to fit on and "ride" the miniature equipment, such as plastic or stuffed animals, dolls, cars, or balls
- paper and drawing materials
- (optional) book about playgrounds, such as *Playgrounds* (by Gail Gibbons)
- (optional) digital camera and printer

Spotlight Vocabulary

- motion
- move
- playground
- equipment
- amusement
- ride
- gravity
- friction
- direction words (such as up, down, back, and forth)
- motion words (such as roll, slide, swing, and spin)
- force words (such as push, pull, lift, and twist)

Begin

1. Review the class graph, book, and bulletin board completed in **Exploration 6: Moving Fun on the Playground**. Share the pictures of the children playing on their favorite piece of playground equipment. Ask the children how things move on the playground and at amusement parks.

2. Have children work in small groups or individually to build miniature playground equipment or amusement rides. The models can depict actual rides or can be brand new inventions. Show the children all the materials that they can use to make their models. Point out the small objects that can "ride" the models. Give children ample time to explore the materials and build their rides.

Designs can be new inventions.

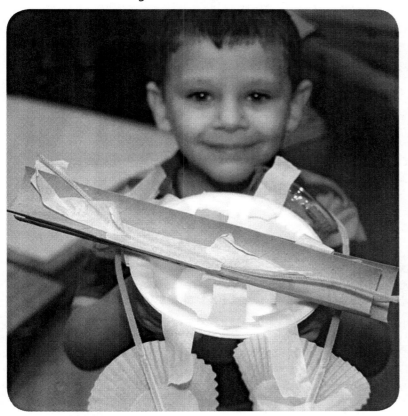

Sci-Lit Connection

You can begin this activity by reading the class a book about playgrounds, such as *Playgrounds* (by Gail Gibbons).

Helpful Hints

- When introducing the materials that are available to the class, model how some of the materials might be used.

- Offering small objects (such as animals, cars, and balls) that can "ride" the miniature rides will help inspire children during the design process.

A seesaw design

Continue

3. When building is complete, have the children show, explain, and demonstrate to the rest of the class how their rides work. If possible, leave the rides assembled so the children can explore each other's designs.

Questions to guide the sharing:

> *How does your ride work?*

> *Does your ride have a name? What is it?*

> *How does the object "ride" your design?*

> *What kind of motion is going on during the ride?*

> *What kind of force makes your ride work?*

Seen and heard:

A child said, "Baby Bear Playground," "Bears slide and go around," and "Push the bear."

4. Have the children draw pictures of their rides to hang on the wall or bulletin board. Photographs can also be taken.

What to Look For

Look for children to discuss different kinds of motion. Children should demonstrate some knowledge of spinning, swinging, sliding, and going up and down. Also look for creative thinking and use of materials. Look for the willingness to modify the construction to make the creation stronger and more usable. As children tell about their creations, listen for words that explain how the rides move.

Application 3:
Bottle Bowling

Children use the knowledge gained about ramps and balls to design ramps that will successfully knock down bowling pins.

Duration

1 large group session

Purpose

- use knowledge of ramps and balls to construct and play a game
- communicate and work cooperatively to design and build a ramp
- modify and retest ramp construction during the game as needed to knock down the bowling pins
- communicate favorite ramp ideas through drawings and words
- cooperatively play the game

What You Need

- poster board or large piece of paper
- masking tape
- variety of objects to make ramps
- ☞ *Offer ramp materials (such as stiff cardboard, foam board, and lightweight wood) and items to prop up the ramps (such as blocks, boxes, and books).*
- variety of materials to modify the ramps
- ☞ *Offer materials such as cardboard tubes, yardsticks, car tracks, and blocks.*
- variety of balls
- empty and clean plastic soft-drink bottles
- ☞ *As an alternative, empty and clean plastic milk jugs or store-bought toy bowling pins can be used.*

- paper and drawing materials

Be Safe

Make sure children do not throw or kick the balls in this game.

Getting Ready

- Prepare a mat as shown at right so children will know where to place the pins each time.
- Decide where in the room to place the "bowling alley." Tape the mat you prepared to the floor.

Spotlight Vocabulary

- ramp
- ball
- build
- knock
- force words (such as roll and gravity)
- direction words (such as up and down)
- speed words (such as fast and slow)

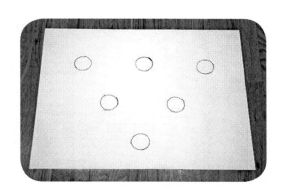

Begin

1. Ask the children what they know about bowling. Demonstrate on the floor how to bowl using a ball and the substitute bowling pins. (Don't use a ramp during this demonstration.) Review different motions (such as roll and slide) and different forces (such as push and stop).

2. Remind the children of all the fun activities that they did with ramps. Model for the children how to set up a ramp.

3. Have children work in small groups to plan, construct, and build a ramp. The ramp will be used to release a ball in order to knock over as many bowling pins as possible. Show the children all the possible materials for making their ramps. Younger children may need more guidance. (See Helpful Hint.)

Helpful Hint

As an alternative to having small groups design ramps, you can do steps 3 and 4 together as a class. Begin by rolling a light ball down a low ramp so that the bowling pins stay up. Ask the class what you should try to successfully knock down the pins. Point out that only one thing should be changed at a time during the redesign process so you know what works and what doesn't work. End with a setup that successfully knocks down the pins. Give time for children to try the setup. Offer time and additional materials for free exploration.

Continue

4. Ask one group to bring their ramp to the designated bowling alley. Have the children select which ball they are going to use. Give the group four tries to knock down all the pins. (The rules of this game can be changed for each particular group or situation.) After each ball roll, children may change their ramp or ball selection in hopes of knocking down the remaining pins. The purpose of the game is to keep trying to find a way to knock down all the pins. (Children need to feel success at constructing and persevering.)

Questions to guide the design process:
> *How did your ramp help knock down the pins?*
> *How can you change your ramp or ball selection to knock down more pins?*

Seen and heard:
Children said, "The ball goes down faster," "Try a bigger box," and "Use three balls."

5. Have children draw pictures showing which ball and ramp they thought was the best setup for knocking down the most pins. Write a brief caption under each picture based on the artist's own words.

What to Look For

Look for children to experiment with different balls and ramp sizes and heights in order to knock down the most pins. Do the children look for ways to make the ball go down faster and harder? Do they explore ways to make the ball head in a different direction? Do they try different plans to make the ramp better?

Stop and Reflect

What you need

- small pieces of paper
- pencils and crayons
- poster board or large sheet of paper

Reflection activity

Give each child a small piece of paper. Ask the children to draw or write one thing that they have learned from all of their investigations.

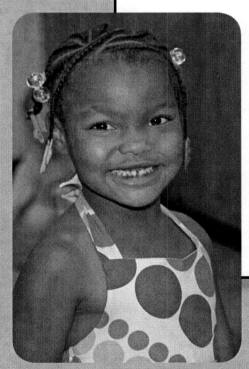

Bring the children together to show their papers and share their discoveries with the class. You may want to sort the papers into several categories as children share. For example, one category could be about ramps and another could be about playground and amusement rides. List the categories on the top of a poster board or large sheet of paper. Children can help you decide in which category each paper belongs. Attach the children's papers to the class chart in the appropriate categories. When all have shared, display this class chart in the room.

Part 6:
Motion Across the Curriculum

How can you use motion across the curriculum?

This section includes fun ideas for extending children's learning about motion into other areas of learning.

Across the Curriculum 1:
Writing to Learn

Children share their thoughts and knowledge about motion with their teacher, classmates, and families by creating pictures and stories that summarize what they learned through observation, exploration, and investigation.

Duration

1 large group session

Purpose

- document ideas about motion
- create pictures to tell about motion
- write stories about motion

What You Need

- paper and drawing materials
- class charts and examples of children's work from previous activities
- (optional) digital camera and printer

Spotlight Vocabulary

Encourage children to use the Spotlight Vocabulary words from previous activities.

Begin

1. Display previous class charts and examples of children's work. Ask children what they learned about motion. Tell children they will be making pages for a class book.

2. Have each child draw a picture showing something he or she learned about motion. Write a brief caption under each picture based on the artist's own words.

3. You can also have children dictate stories based on what they learned. You may have several children contribute to a longer story or individual children tell their own stories. Encourage children to use

Helpful Hint

Meet with the children in small groups to improve participation and individual contributions.

the Spotlight Vocabulary words from previous activities. If available, use a digital camera and printer to quickly add pictures of children and their work to the stories.

4. Assemble the pictures and stories into a class book. Remember to create a title and include children's names as authors.

Continue

5. Gather the children together and read the class book aloud. Highlight children's illustrations and contributions. Place the class book in the reading center for free exploration.

What to Look For

Watch for children to describe what they learned while exploring motion and working with objects that can be moved. Listen for them to include Spotlight Vocabulary words in their descriptions. Encourage the children to recall and articulate details from their experiences.

Helpful Hint

You can make copies of the class book for children to take home. This empowers children to see the results of their work and to share their ideas just like scientists do. It also provides a valuable learning link between your classroom and children's homes.

Across the Curriculum 2:
Book Adventures

Children learn more about motion by exploring children's literature.

Duration

several large group sessions

Purpose

- participate in a kinesthetic demonstration
- draw pictures of vehicles and other things that move
- discover common ideas about motion in literature
- find out new information through literature

What You Need

- book about a train
- paper and drawing materials
- selection of both fiction and nonfiction children's books on vehicles, other things that move, and motion

Spotlight Vocabulary

- motion   • information
- story   • read

Helpful Hint

Here are just a few book ideas:

- *Freight Train* (by Donald Crews)
- *The Little Engine That Could* (by Watty Piper)
- *Go, Dog, Go* (by P.D. Eastman)
- *Stop That Ball* (by Mike McClintlock)
- *Carousel* (by Donald Crews)

Begin

1. Read a book about a train to the class. Point out that trains have wheels so they can roll on train tracks.

2. Divide the children in groups of four. Have each group stand in a line to make a "train." The first person in each line is the engine and the last person is the caboose. Ask the "engines" to lead their trains around the room. Have children use sound effects such as whistles, chug chugs, and choo choos. Rotate the children so everyone has a chance to be the engine. Add additional fun by having the children act out events from the story.

3. Have children draw pictures of trains. Be sure they include wheels in their pictures.

Continue

4. Take several large group sessions to read aloud additional books about motion, vehicles, and other things that move. Discuss how each book relates to motion. Have children act out the motions and draw the motion objects. Afterwards, make the books available for free exploration.

What to Look For

Through acting out and drawing pictures, watch for children to understand the motion of trains and other things that move. Look for children to demonstrate through discussion their awareness that literature can reinforce experiences and offer new ideas.

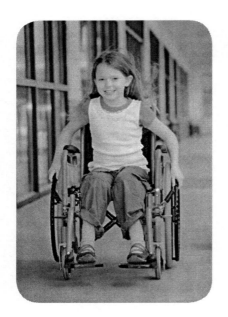

Across the Curriculum 3:
Wheels That Help

Children explore the use and importance of wheels to people who rely on wheelchairs to move around.

Duration

1 large group session

Purpose

- listen to a story related to the activity
- explore the importance of wheelchairs and ramps to people with disabilities
- gain a better appreciation and understanding of the challenges and accomplishments of people with physical disabilities

What You Need

- book about someone using a wheelchair, such as *Mama Zooms* (by Jane Cowen-Fletcher)
- wheelchair or wheeled device such as rolling office chair, stroller, wagon, or grocery cart
- ramps or other specifically designed accessible areas in and around the school

Be Safe

Supervise the children as they roll and move in the wheelchair.

Getting Ready

If possible, invite a person who uses a wheelchair to discuss with the children the importance of a wheelchair and how it works.

Spotlight Vocabulary

- wheelchair
- disability
- ramp
- force words (such as push and pull)
- motion words (such as roll and spin)
- direction words (such as up and down)

Begin

1. Read the class a storybook about someone using a wheelchair, such as *Mama Zooms* (by Jane Cowen-Fletcher).

2. Discuss how some people who cannot walk use a wheelchair to get from place to place. People in wheelchairs use ramps or elevators instead of stairs. With careful supervision, have children use a wheelchair or similar device to experience ramps, sidewalks, playgrounds, and other areas of the school.

   Questions to guide the observing process:
   > *How does it feel to be in a wheelchair?*
   > *What is easy about being in a wheelchair? What is hard?*

Continue

3. If possible, arrange for a person who uses a wheelchair to come to the classroom and tell the children about his or her daily activities. The guest can tell the children about some challenges that he or she may also have. Discuss how important the wheels are to the movement of the chair. Why are ramps used in the parking lot or sidewalk? Why are there special areas in the rest room or parking lot for the use of wheelchairs?

4. Have the children list the many things that someone in a wheelchair can do.

What to Look For

Look for the children to understand that, although some people might need wheelchairs to move, they can still do many things, go many places, and feel the same way that a person not in a wheelchair can feel. Children should realize that there are special adaptations made in and around buildings (such as ramps and larger rest room areas) so that people who use wheelchairs will be able to move more easily.

Across the Curriculum 4:
Fun and Games

Children play different games related to motion to reinforce what they've learned.

Duration
several large group sessions

Purpose
- apply knowledge of how objects move while playing a game
- spell simple words while playing a game
- apply knowledge about wheels and wheeled objects while playing games

What You Need
- ball if playing the Hot Potato Game
- wheeled toy if playing the Tell a Story Game or the Name That Wheeled Object Game
- class chart from **Exploration 5: Wheel Day** if playing the Name That Wheeled Object Game

Spotlight Vocabulary
Encourage children to use the Spotlight Vocabulary words from previous activities.

Name That Wheeled Object Game

1. Display the **Exploration 5: Wheel Day** class chart. Sit in a circle with the children. Name something that has wheels. Roll a wheeled toy to a child who has to name something else that has wheels. After that child names a wheeled object, he or she pushes the toy across the circle to another child.

2. Continue the game until everyone has a turn.

Move Along Game

1. Begin outside with all the children standing with you at one end of the playground. Say a phrase that describes a type of movement (for example, "trains chugging," "boats sailing," or "tops spinning"). Have the children pretend to be the object and act out the movement as they move to the other end of the playground.

2. Have the children turn back towards you. Say another phrase and have the children act out the movement as they come towards you. The children can repeat moving from one end of the playground to the other, acting out movements as they go.

Hot Potato Game

1. While sitting in a circle, have the children roll a ball across the circle from person to person as you play music. When the music stops, the person holding the ball stands up and bounces the ball four times as the class spells "roll" (or any other word you choose).

2. Have the standing person sit down and roll the ball to another person in the circle as you begin to play the music again. Repeat step 1 until everyone gets a chance to bounce the ball.

Tell a Story Game

1. Sit in a circle with the children. Begin telling a story about something that has wheels. After a few sentences, stop and roll a wheeled toy to one of the children. That child can either add more to the story or roll the toy to another person. If the child adds something to the story, he or she should roll the toy to another child after saying a few sentences.

2. As each child gets the toy, he or she can choose to add more to the story or roll it to another person.

Across the Curriculum 5:
Motion in Art

Children experience motion as they do fun art projects.

Duration
several large and small group sessions

Purpose
- discover that art can be created by the movement of marbles and wheels
- match tire prints to toy vehicles

What You Need
- child-safe, washable paint
- paper suitable for painting on
- plastic plates to hold paint
- boxes with lids (such as small shoe boxes) and marbles if doing Marble Painting
- different plastic vehicles with rolling wheels if doing Wheel Painting
- crayons/markers and rubber bands/tape if doing Draw Through Driving

Getting Ready
- For Wheel Painting, make tire prints by rolling different plastic vehicles in paint and then over small pieces of paper. Use a separate piece of paper for each vehicle. Let dry.
- For Draw Through Driving, use rubber bands or tape to attach crayons or markers to the back of plastic cars or trucks.

Spotlight Vocabulary
- marble
- paint
- wheel
- tracks
- movement
- draw

Marble Painting

Tape a piece of paper to the inside bottom of a box. Have a child dip a few marbles into paint and drop the marbles into the box. The child can close the lid and shake. (As an alternative, tape a piece of paper on the inside of a box lid. Have child dip a few marbles into paint and drop the marbles into the lid. The child can move the box lid around to make the paint-coated marbles roll around on the paper.)

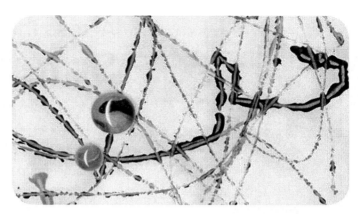

Wheel Painting

Cover a table with a large piece of paper. Have children roll plastic vehicles through paint and then over the paper to make tracks and marks. When the paper is dry, have children try to identify the toy that made each track. Next, show children the tire prints you made in Getting Ready and ask children to match vehicles with corresponding prints.

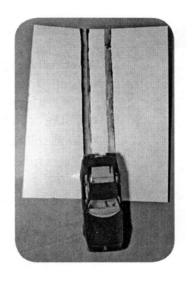 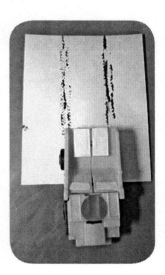

Draw Through Driving

Have the children "drive" the wheeled toys with attached crayons or markers (see Getting Ready) over paper. The marks show the paths of the vehicles around the paper.

Across the Curriculum 6:
Safety in Motion

Children learn about seat belt and helmet safety.

Duration

1 large group session

Purpose

- learn the importance of wearing seat belts by watching a demonstration with a ramp, wheeled object, and "passenger"
- review the movement of bicycles, bicycle safety, and the importance of wearing helmets

What You Need

- ramp
- ☞ *You can prop up stiff cardboard or a wooden board with books, blocks, or boxes.*
- large, solid object (such as a book or wall)
- object to act as a passenger (such as small doll or stuffed animal)
- vehicle capable of holding the "passenger"
- something to act as a seat belt (such as string, shoestring, or ribbon)
- bicycle helmet
- playground ball that fits inside a bicycle helmet
- (optional) bicycles/tricycles and helmets brought from home

Getting Ready

- Set up a ramp in front of a solid object (such as a book or wall) as shown below. Set the proper ramp height for steps 1–3 by practicing with the vehicle and the passenger.

- You may want to invite a police officer or other guest to talk about seat belt, bicycle, and helmet safety.

Spotlight Vocabulary
- solid
- stop
- seat belt
- safety
- helmet
- pedal
- speed words (such as slow and fast)

Begin

1. Ask the children what will happen if a vehicle is released at the top of the ramp. Demonstrate that the vehicle hits the solid object and stops.

2. Place the "passenger" on the vehicle and ask the children what will happen if the vehicle with passenger is released at the top of the ramp. Demonstrate that the vehicle stops when it hits the solid object and the passenger flies off the vehicle. Repeat several times.

3. Ask the children what you can do to keep the passenger from falling off the vehicle. Encourage the children to suggest tieing the passenger on the vehicle like seat belts hold people in cars. Make a "seat belt" for the passenger and demonstrate that the seat belt holds the passenger on the vehicle when the vehicle stops at the end of the ramp. Repeat rolling the vehicle down the ramp several times.

   Questions to guide the discussion:
   > *How can we keep the passenger from falling off?*
   > *How do we stay safe when riding in cars?*

4. Discuss the importance of wearing a seat belt when riding in a car. Inviting a police officer or other guest to talk about seat belt safety could make the lesson more memorable.

Continue

5. Gather the children in a circle. Ask the class if bicycles move by themselves. What do we need to do to make bicycles move? Prompt the children to say that we need to pedal bicycles to make them move.

6. Have the children lie down on their backs on the floor. Ask them to lift their legs into the air and pretend to pedal a bicycle. Point out that their legs move in circles as they "pedal." Have them pedal slower and faster.

7. Demonstrate the importance of wearing a helmet when riding a bicycle by showing the children a playground ball. Press on the ball to show that the ball changes its shape. Place the ball in the helmet. Press on the helmet and explain that the helmet doesn't change its shape and the ball inside stays protected.

8. Ask the children to list bicycle safety rules and add rules as needed. Inviting a bicycle patrol officer or other guest to talk about helmet and bicycle safety could make the lesson more memorable.

Helpful Hint

Recite the poem "Humpty Dumpty." Discuss how a helmet might have kept Humpty Dumpty safe.

Questions to guide the discussion:

> *How can people stay safe while riding bicycles?*

> *What can people wear to protect themselves while riding bicycles?*

> *How does wearing a helmet keep you safer?*

Part 7:
Science
for Young
Learners

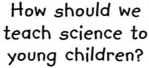

How should we
teach science to
young children?

This section contains information
on developmentally appropriate
science instruction for young
children, including fundamental
concepts and process skills,
inquiry-based science, teaching
with learning cycles, and
documenting children's learning.

Why Early Childhood Science?

Why bother with science in early childhood? Young children can't memorize the geologic periods or understand chemical reactions. Learning ABCs and how to share, listen, and even tie shoes, is challenging stuff! Plus, the school day is too short to accomplish all we have to do now. Why not wait until children are older to introduce science?

The National Science Education Standards emphasize that all children can learn science and that all children should have the opportunity to become scientifically literate. In *Science in Early Childhood: Developing and Acquiring Fundamental Concepts and Skills,* Karen Lind writes "In order for this learning to happen, the effort to introduce children to the essential experiences of science inquiry and explorations must begin at an early age." (Lind, 1999)

Reaching Potentials: Transforming Early Childhood Curriculum and Assessment (from the National Association for the Education of Young Children) summarizes what developmentally-appropriate science instruction for young children is…and is not. The authors use the term "sciencing" to convey the child's active involvement in learning about science and to emphasize process in effective science teaching.

Process Skill Power

"Concepts are the building blocks of knowledge; they allow people to organize and categorize information. During early childhood, children actively engage in acquiring fundamental concepts and in learning fundamental process skills."

Karen Lind, 1999

For Children 3 through 8, Developmentally Appropriate Sciencing…	
Is	**Is Not**
actively participating	memorizing a lot of facts
handling materials controlling their own actions	watching the teacher do most of the demonstrating and handling of objects
investigating familiar phenomena	studying content with no link to their knowledge or experience
reflecting on teachers' open-ended questions	being restricted by closed, single-right-answer questioning or being told what to expect
observing the results of their own actions	lacking opportunities to observe the results of their own actions
experiencing both planned and spontaneous opportunities	experiencing science only as teacher-planned activities
investigating and working individually or in small groups	participating in science activities only in a large group
investigating the range of basic concepts	learning about only one or two concepts
exploring a variety of content from life, earth, and physical sciences	learning only limited content
having their knowledge and skill assessed in multiple ways	having their knowledge and skills assessed only by written tests

Reaching Potentials: Transforming Early Childhood Curriculum and Assessment, Vol 2. "Transforming Science Curriculum," 1995, S. Kilmer and H. Hofman, pg. 62. Reproduced with permission of the National Association for the Education of Young Children.

When presented in a way that is meaningful for young minds, early childhood science education provides the foundation for a lifetime of science learning both in and out of school. The goal of the *Big Science for Little Hands* series is to help young children develop an understanding of fundamental concepts about the physical world and the fundamental process skills suitable for their developmental level.

Fundamental Concepts

The fundamental concepts allow children to organize their experiences with the physical world into meaningful patterns—the beginning of true science learning. How do children develop an awareness of these fundamental concepts? They need repeated, personal experiences with materials and events from their everyday world and the tools—in the form of process skills—to help them make sense of these experiences and the world around them.

The activities in this book provide a specific progression of experiences that help children build an understanding of the fundamental concepts listed below. This progression is in the form of a learning cycle. (See page 142 for a discussion of learning cycles.)

Fundamental Concepts	
Fundamental Concepts about the Physical World for the Early Childhood Level	**Examples of Use in Activities**
Objects and events have observable characteristics.	In **Awareness 2: Getting Excited About Motion Toys,** children learn that objects have observable characteristics as they explore how different toys move in certain ways.
A person can act on objects or materials to change them and observe the results of their action.	In **Inquiry 1: Raise the Ramp,** children find that increasing the incline of a ramp will cause a toy car to travel further.
The physical world has patterns that help a person predict what will happen next.	By the time they reach **Application 3: Bottle Bowling,** children have observed patterns of events that help them decide how to build and modify a ramp to successfully knock down "bowling pins."

Fundamental Process Skills

Each activity in this book helps children develop one or more of the process skills appropriate for the early childhood level. How we define these process skills is important, because what one person understands to be "measuring" or "organizing" may not be developmentally appropriate for this level. Review the following list and definitions carefully. Note that young children can begin practicing simpler versions of intermediate-level process skills.

Process Skills	
Fundamental Process Skills for the Early Childhood Level	
Observing	Using the senses to gather information about objects or events is the most fundamental of the scientific thinking processes. Rich observation experiences enable children to create a repertoire of possible properties that make up objects or events and form a foundation for comparing and organizing.
Communicating	Sharing oral or written ideas and descriptions in a way that helps others understand the meaning.
Comparing	Examining the character of objects in order to discover similarities or differences. Comparing builds upon the process of observing and begins in younger children with comparing two objects at a time.
Measuring	Comparing objects to arbitrary units that may or may not be standardized. Measuring skills begin to develop as children compare objects to one another (such as bigger/smaller, hotter/colder). The skill then extends to comparing objects to nonstandard units of measure (such as one block equals three counting bears). Beginning in primary grades, children can understand the value of using standard units such as pounds and inches.
Organizing	This skill includes grouping, classifying, seriating (ordering objects along a continuum), and sequencing (placing events one after another so that they tell a logical story). • Grouping begins at about age 3 with resemblance sorting: putting objects together (in pairs, piles, or chains) on the basis of one-to-one correspondence. Each pair or pile may be grouped based on a different kind of resemblance, such as red objects in one pile and square ones in another. • Consistent and exhaustive sorting starts at about age 6, when a child will use up all the pieces in a set using one consistent rule for grouping, such as color. • Multiple membership classifying—the ability to place an object into more than one category at the same time or into one category based on two or more simultaneous properties—begins at about age 8.
Simple Versions of Intermediate Process Skills for Early Childhood Children	
Reasonable guessing	More than a simple guess, based on prior knowledge. For example, perceiving a pattern emerging and surmising how it will continue. Reasonable guessing is a step towards predicting.
Early data collecting and interpreting	Can include counting and making pictures to represent information discovered by exploration. Children can reflect upon these results together. Teachers can model these process skills with the children as ways to organize information found in exploration and investigation. This skill gives purpose to activities and further experiments.

Facilitating "Sciencing"

Spontaneous sciencing occurs every day. Whenever children see something of interest, wonder about it, and investigate to answer their questions, science is going on. Scheduled opportunities build upon these spontaneous experiences, enriching the active sciencing that comes naturally to children.

Teachers are the role models and facilitators of sciencing. As models, teachers need to display all of the behaviors identified as outcomes for the children. "Teachers are not expected to know all there is to know about sciencing. What is important is that the teacher be open, enthusiastic, and willing to wonder 'What happens if...?'" (Kilmer, 1995)

Science learning flourishes when teachers facilitate a classroom atmosphere that respects each child's contribution, supports inquiry and experimentation without passing judgement about right and wrong, and embraces "mistakes" as opportunities for new discoveries. Strategic comments and questions can focus and extend children's thinking. By carefully observing a child's behavior, teachers can help put into words an unspoken question a child may be thinking about.

One effective technique for helping children try new approaches to investigations is to join the child in an activity and begin by imitating what the child is doing. The adult then gradually adds something new to his or her actions. "If, for instance, the focus is on bubbles, after the child has had time to explore blowing bubbles in various ways but has not spontaneously used some of the different bubble-makers provided, the teacher sits beside the child. After using the same bubble-maker as the child is using, the teacher begins to try different ones." (Kilmer, 1995) Frequently, the child will notice the teacher's behavior and expand his or her own exploration.

> ## Process Skill Power
>
> "Children who have many interesting, direct experiences over time with science concepts will gradually understand the broader principles as they develop the cognitive skills to make more abstract generalizations."
>
> Sally Kilmer and Helenmarie Hofman, 1995

Self-Directed Inquiry

As children develop and practice the process skills and inquiry modeled by the teacher, their abilities to initiate, plan, and conduct self-directed inquiry grow. Children "begin the process of asking and answering their own questions, which is at the heart of the inquiry experience." (Villavicencio, 2000)

Joanna Villavicencio's experiences doing self-directed inquiry with 4- and 5-year-old children show that young children benefit from these opportunities. As children explore, she guides them to follow a five-part structure that helps organize their investigations:
- form a question;
- make a plan;
- do the investigation;
- record and report; and
- reflect, revisit, and plan again.

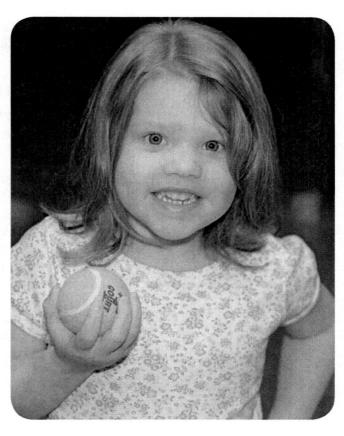

Until they have experience with inquiry, children often have difficulty asking questions that can be tested. Teachers need to actively facilitate children's efforts to ask such questions. Wendy Cheong writes, "While watching the children explore, I encourage them to ask questions about whatever seems curious to them...I support them in various ways. For example, I model techniques and ask a lot of open-ended questions, such as: 'Can you tell me what you are trying to find out with this instrument?' Eventually, the children get used to hearing the kinds of questions that can lead to investigations." (Cheong, 2000)

Jane Bresnik models this process by asking questions that begin with "I wonder," such as "I wonder what will happen if I hold the ramp higher?" The words "I wonder..." become the first part of a template Jane uses to help children organize their investigations. Children state their "I wonder" question, explain their plan, conduct their tests, and then explain what happened using the "I found out..." prompt. (Bresnik, 2000)

As children begin their investigations, teachers need to work with them by observing, questioning, supporting their efforts, and redirecting their investigations. Reporting the results of investigations to others is an important step. Joanna Villavicencio explains that "In the beginning, the children have a hard time articulating their discoveries, so I help them find the right words to explain what they discovered...I have seen how language develops during the inquiry process. As children share what they see, they find words to express and refine their thinking." (Villavicencio, 2000)

How Children Learn

Research on how humans learn helps educators understand what fosters learning and how to improve ineffective or even detrimental aspects of teaching.

The brain needs data it can use to construct knowledge. Our senses are like windows that allow the brain to collect and store data with everything we do, perceive, think, or feel. "Learners do not simply mirror what they are told or what they read. The brain does not store a picture of an event. It does not directly record anything that is shown." (Lowery, 1998) What the brain does do is store information clustered into different areas of the brain with networks of pathways connecting these places. For example, sensory perceptions are grouped in different places in the brain—shapes, colors, movements, textures, and aromas are each stored in their own places. Components of language are also stored in their own places—nouns in one place, verbs in another.

"As the brain constructs connections among brain cells, it connects the organization of words, objects, events, and relationships...The result is that human knowledge is stored in clusters and organized within the brain into systems that people use to interpret familiar situations and reason about new ones." (Lowery, 1998) The more avenues that children have to receive data through the senses, the more connections their brains will make.

Knowledge is constructed through experience, but the quality of that construction is greatly affected by how well the brain organizes and stores relationships. For example, a child exploring a magnet experiences the following relationships:

- a relationship between the learner and the object (how the hand and arm are positioned to hold the magnet);
- cause and effect relationships between the learner's actions and observed results (how the magnet can be moved and manipulated); and
- cause and effect relationships in an interaction between objects in the environment (how other objects behave in the presence of the magnet).

As exploration continues, "learners try to link new perceptions to what they have already constructed in the brain's storage systems. They use this prior knowledge to interpret the new material in terms of established knowledge." (Lowery, 1998) Bits of information that are not integrated with prior knowledge are forgotten. The more opportunities children have to explore relationships among objects and ideas and to use their prior knowledge, the richer and more permanent their constructions of knowledge will be. This is accomplished through rehearsals—reinforcing what has been learned while adding something new.

The activities in this book have been thoughtfully constructed to address what we know about how children learn. Doing these activities with young children will help to build a foundation for a lifetime of science learning and exploration.

Find Out More

Bredekamp, Sue, and Teresa Rosegrant, Eds. ***Reaching Potentials: Appropriate Curriculum and Assessment for Young Children.*** Vol. 1. Washington, DC: National Association for the Education of Young Children (NAEYC), 1992.

Bredekamp, Sue, and Teresa Rosegrant, Eds. ***Reaching Potentials: Transforming Early Childhood Curriculum and Assessment.*** Vol. 2. Washington, DC: National Association for the Education of Young Children (NAEYC), 1995.

Connect: Inquiry Learning Issue Vol. 13(4), 2000: pgs. 1–26.

Dialogue on Early Childhood Science, Mathematics, and Technology Education; American Association for the Advancement of Science (AAAS) Project 2061: Washington, DC, 1999.

Lind, Karen. ***Exploring Science in Early Childhood: A Developmental Approach.*** Albany, NY: Delmar Publishers, 2000.

Lowery, Lawrence. **"How New Science Curriculums Reflect Brain Research."** *Educational Leadership* Vol. 56(3), 1998: pgs. 26–30.

Lowery, Lawrence. ***The Scientific Thinking Process.*** Berkeley, CA: Lawrence Hall of Science, 1992.

National Association for the Education of Young Children (NAEYC). ***Developmentally Appropriate Practice in Early Childhood Programs Serving Children from Birth through Age 8.*** 1997. Available: www.naeyc.org/about/positions/daptoc.asp (accessed September 9, 2008).

National Research Council. ***National Science Education Standards: Observe, Interact, Change, Learn.*** Washington, DC: National Academy Press, 1996.

Good Science at Any Age

The list below was developed by teachers and administrators participating in the Vermont Elementary Science Project. They write, "The intent is not to use this guide as a checklist, but as a statement of what we value in the areas of science processes, science dispositions, and science concept development. We urge you to capture evidence of your own students engaging in these indicators."

Inquiry-Based Science: What Does It Look Like?

When students are doing inquiry-based science, an observer will see that

Children view themselves as scientists in the process of learning.

- Children look forward to doing science.
- They demonstrate a desire to learn more.
- They seek to collaborate and work cooperatively with their peers.
- They are confident in doing science; they demonstrate a willingness to modify ideas, take risks, and display healthy skepticism.

Children accept an "invitation to learn" and readily engage in the exploration process.

- Children exhibit curiosity and ponder observations.
- They move around, selecting and using the materials they need.
- They take the opportunity and the time to try out their own ideas.

Children plan and carry out investigations.

- Children design a way to try out their ideas, not expecting to be told what to do.
- They plan ways to verify, extend, or discard ideas.
- They carry out investigations by handling materials, observing, measuring, and recording data.

Children communicate using a variety of methods.

- Children express ideas in a variety of ways, such as with journals, reporting, drawing, graphing, and charting.
- They listen, speak, and write about science with parents, teachers, and peers.
- They use the language of the processes of science.
- They communicate their level of understanding of concepts that they have developed to date.

Children propose explanations and solutions and build a store of concepts.

- Children offer explanations from a store of previous knowledge.
- They use investigations to answer their own questions.
- They sort information and decide what information is important.
- They are willing to revise explanations as they gain new knowledge.

Children raise questions.

- Children ask questions (verbally or through actions).
- They use questions to lead them to investigations that generate further questions or ideas.
- They value and enjoy asking questions as an important part of science.

Children use observation.

- Children observe, as opposed to just looking.
- They see details; they detect sequences and events; they notice changes, similarities, and differences.
- They make connections to previously held ideas.

Children critique their science practices.

- They use indicators to assess their own work.
- They report their strengths and weaknesses.
- They reflect with their peers.

The Vermont Elementary Science Project (VESP), Trinity College, Burlington, VT 05401; (802) 658-3664; awarded to The NETWORK, Inc., Andover, MA, by the National Science Foundation.

Adapted from *Connect*, March–April 1995, pg. 13. Reproduced with permission of Synergy Learning.

Teaching with Learning Cycles

What are learning cycles and why teach with them? A learning cycle is a structured approach to science teaching that takes into account what we know about how children learn. The work of researchers such as Piaget, Vygotsky, and Lowery has taught us that children acquire new concepts and skills by building upon what they already know and are able to do. This process is called the construction of knowledge.

In *Guidelines for Appropriate Curriculum Content and Assessment in Programs Serving Children Ages 3 through 8,* the National Association for the Education of Young Children (NAEYC) recommends that "the curriculum provides conceptual frameworks for children so that their mental constructions based on prior knowledge become more complex over time." (NAEYC, 1990)

Often, the early childhood science curriculum consists of conceptually unrelated activities chosen to coordinate with the seasons of the year or some other theme. NAEYC encourages science curriculum that builds conceptually upon itself rather than only coordinating with such a theme: "As in menu planning, the individual recipes may be appropriate and valuable, but without a framework and organization, they may fail to provide the opportunity for rich conceptual development that is likely with a more coherent, thoughtful approach."

Providing this "coherent, thoughtful approach" can be a challenge, but the structure of a learning cycle gives teachers a framework for doing so. In *How New Science Curriculums Reflect Brain Research,* Lawrence Lowery explains, "The learning cycle is viewed as a way to take students on a quest for knowledge that leads to the construction of knowledge. It is used both as a curriculum development procedure and a teaching strategy." A learning cycle creates a sequence of instructions that provides "a rehearsal of prior knowledge constructions, thus making them more permanent, and provides something new that the brain can assimilate into its prior construction, thus enriching and extending those constructions."

Typically, a learning cycle has four phases, each with one or more activities. The phases of the learning cycle are summarized on the following pages. This summary is adapted from NAEYC's *Guidelines for Appropriate Curriculum Content and Assessment in Programs Serving Children Ages 3 through 8.*

Process Skill Power

"The sequence of... instruction is important to move children from being novices to becoming experts. Each new challenge does two things: provides a rehearsal of prior knowledge constructions, thus making them more permanent, and provides something new that the brain can assimilate into its prior construction, thus enriching and extending those constructions."

Lawrence Lowery, 1998

Phase 1: Awareness—What's in my world? What do I know?

The awareness phase helps children develop broad recognition of the parameters of the learning—events, objects, people, or concepts.

During awareness, children
- experience,
- awaken curiosity, and
- develop an interest.

The teacher's role is to
- create a rich environment;
- provide opportunities by introducing new objects, people, events, or concepts;
- invite and encourage interest by posing a problem or question;
- respond to children's interest; and
- show interest and enthusiasm.

Phase 2: Exploration—What more can I find out about my world?

The exploration phase enables children to construct personal meaning through sensory experiences with objects, people, events, or concepts.

During exploration, children
- observe and explore materials,
- collect information, and
- construct their own understandings and meanings from their experiences.

The teacher's role is to
- facilitate, support, and enhance exploration;
- ask open-ended questions;
- respect children's thinking and rule systems;
- allow for constructive error; and
- model ways to organize information from experiences.

Phase 3: Inquiry—How can I research new things?

The inquiry phase of the learning cycle enables children to deepen and refine their understanding.

During inquiry, children
- examine,
- investigate,
- propose explanations,
- compare own thinking with that of others,
- generalize, and
- relate to prior learning.

The teacher's role is to
- help children refine understanding,
- ask more focused questions,
- provide information when requested, and
- help children make connections among prior experiences and their investigations.

Phase 4: Application—How can I apply what I learn?

In the application phase, learners apply and use their understandings in new settings and situations. The activities in this phase can also serve as assessment tools.

During application, children
- use their learning in different ways,
- represent learning in various ways,
- apply learning to new situations, and
- formulate new hypotheses and repeat learning cycle.

The teacher's role is to
- create links for application in the world outside the classroom,
- help children apply learning to new situations, and
- provide meaningful situations in which children use what they have learned.

Throughout the learning cycle, open-ended questions encourage the child to put into words what he or she is observing, doing, and wondering. When teaching with a learning cycle, teachers can ask focusing questions to support each phase of the learning cycle.

Find Out More

Barman, Charles R. "**Teaching Teachers: The Learning Cycle.**" *Science and Children* Vol. 26(7), 1989: pgs. 30–32.

Beisenherz, Paul C. "**Explore, Invent, and Apply.**" *Science and Children* Vol. 28(4), 1991: pgs. 30–32.

Marek, Edmund A., and Ann M. L. Cavallo. *The Learning Cycle: Elementary School Science and Beyond.* Portsmouth, NH: Heinemann, 1997.

National Association of Early Childhood Specialists in State Departments of Education (NAECS/SDE). *Guidelines for Appropriate Curriculum Content and Assessment in Programs Serving Children Ages 3 through 8.* Produced jointly with NAECS/SDE and the NAEYC and adopted by both Associations in 1990. Published in *Young Children,* March 1991, pp. 21–38 and in *Reaching Potentials: Appropriate Curriculum and Assessment for Young Children,* Volume 1, 1991, pp. 9–27. Available: *naecs.crc.uiuc.edu/position/currcont.html* (accessed September 9, 2008).

Documenting Learning

The book *Windows on Learning: Documenting Young Children's Work* (Helm, Beneke, and Steinheimer, 1998) begins with this idea: "Documenting children's learning may be one of the most valuable skills a teacher can develop today." In the internationally known preprimary schools of Reggio Emilia, Italy, documentation of children's experience is a standard part of classroom practice. "Documentation practices in Reggio Emilia preprimary schools provide inspiring examples of the importance of displaying children's work with great care and attention to both the content and aesthetic aspects of the display." (Katz, 1996)

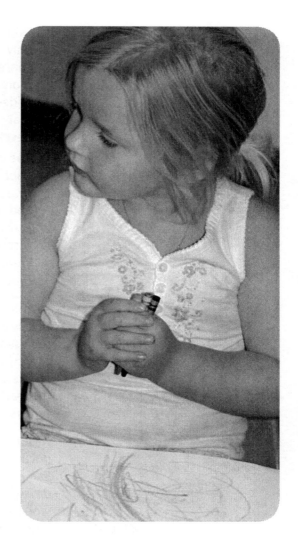

Through documentation, teachers help themselves and others see and understand the learning that is taking place. Documentation serves many purposes, providing

- evidence for monitoring each child's growth and development and reliably assessing progress;
- a method of meeting accountability requirements and communicating with parents and administrators;
- evidence to the child of the importance of his or her work to teachers and parents;
- a means of sharing results with children and capturing their interest;
- opportunities to enhance children's memory of their prior work; and
- a mechanism for teachers to evaluate and improve curriculum and teaching methods, thus becoming producers of research.

"Documenting Early Science Learning" (Jones and Courtney, 2002) recommends that documentation and assessment of children's work in science follow a five-stage cycle. Teachers begin by identifying science objectives: what children should experience, explore, and understand. Next, teachers collect evidence of children's learning according to three guiding principles:

- **Variety of forms of evidence.** Children vary in how they demonstrate their understanding. Types of evidence collected in early childhood classrooms usually include drawings, some with comments dictated to the teacher; photographs; and a record of children's language, particularly in response to open-ended questions.

- **Evidence over a period of time.** A single piece of evidence captures only one moment in time. However, children's understandings of big concepts are not established with a single experience. At a particular moment, a child may be struggling with an idea or question. When added to evidence collected over a period of weeks or months, that single piece of evidence becomes part of a larger picture of development.

- **The understanding of groups of children as well as individuals.** Capturing group conversations at the introduction of a topic can give teachers a sense of what prior experiences, understandings, and misconceptions the group as a whole shares. Science is a social activity, where the sharing of questions, methods, and results is an essential part of the process. Through this sharing, the class as a whole comes to new understandings about a concept. Recording group conversations at the end of a unit can document this outcome.

After collecting evidence of children's learning, the teacher looks closely at the material collected and describes the knowledge represented by the evidence. Doing this step without judgment (such as focusing on what is missing or incorrect) takes practice. Now the children's work can be compared to the standards and goals that the teacher previously identified. Finally, this new information and understanding help the teacher improve instruction and curriculum.

Some early childhood programs use established methods for documentation and assessment. One popular method is the Work Sampling System. It consists of three complementary components: developmental guidelines and checklists, portfolios of children's work, and summary reports by teachers. Assessment takes place three times a year and is meant to place children's work within a broad, developmental perspective. Training to use this system helps teachers develop skills in nonjudgmental recording of behavior. The structure of the system helps teachers organize the collection and evaluation of children's work.

Find Out More

Gandini, Lella. "**Fundamentals of the Reggio Emilia Approach to Early Childhood Education.**" *Young Children* Vol. 49(1), 1993: pgs. 4–8.

Helm, Judy, Sallee Beneke, and Kathy Steinheimer. ***Windows on Learning: Documenting Young Children's Work.*** New York: Teachers College Press, 1998.

Hoisington, Cynthia. "**Using Photographs to Support Children's Science Inquiry.**" *Young Children* Vol. 57(5), 2002: pgs. 26–32.

Jones, Jacqueline, and Rosalea Courtney. "**Documenting Early Science Learning.**" *Young Children* Vol. 57(5), 2002: pgs. 34–40.

Katz, Lilian G. "**Impressions of Reggio Emilia Preschools.**" *Young Children* Vol. 45(6), 1990: pgs. 10–11.

Meisels, S.J., et al. ***An Overview: The Work Sampling System.*** Ann Arbor, MI: Rebus Planning Associates, 1994.

Part 8:
All About
Motion

What are some interesting facts about motion?

This section briefly summarizes the science of motion. You may choose to share some of this information with the children when appropriate during the class sessions.

Our World Is Constantly in Motion

As an integral part of everyday life, motion is an important concept in early childhood education. By learning about how things move, children begin to understand more about the world around them.

Objects do not move by themselves—a force (a push or a pull) must be applied to make them move. The forces of pushing and pulling can change the position and motion of an object. An object usually moves in the direction that it is pushed or pulled. Once something is moving, it will continue moving until some kind of force stops it.

Objects move in different ways as forces act upon them. Balls roll. Tops spin. Swings move back and forth. Some objects move quickly and some move slowly. Children can observe and describe how different objects move and can begin to classify objects by how they move. They can also act as scientists as they explore ways to change, control, and predict the motion of objects when they are pushed or pulled.

The playground environment is the perfect place for children to experience, explore, and observe the forces of pushing and pulling and how these forces affect objects and people. Children can become "motionologists" and learn basic science concepts while playing and having fun on the slide, swing, merry-go-round, and seesaw.

The following brief sections provide some information about the science concepts behind the activities in this book. While your children are not ready for this level of content, you may feel more confident in your teaching if you understand a bit more of the science.

Gravity

Gravity is a force that acts at a distance, unlike a "contact" force that we might use to push a toy car across the floor. When an object falls to the ground, it does so because of gravity, a force of attraction that exists between the mass of the object and the mass of the earth. These two masses pull each other. We don't usually think of the falling object contributing to the force of gravity, because when an object, such as an apple, is dropped, the apple moves but the earth does not. The reason the earth does not move is that it is so much more massive than the apple.

Mass and Weight

The activities in this book use the term "weight" rather than "mass" because the distinction between mass and weight is outside the realm of young children's understanding. A balance actually measures mass, which is the quantity of matter in an object. Even though we sometimes use the terms heavy and light when referring to mass, mass is not the same thing as weight. Mass is a characteristic property of the object, but weight is not.

The weight of an object is the gravitational force that the earth exerts on an object. An object's weight depends on the mass of the object and its location. For instance, the weight of an object will vary slightly if it is moved from sea level to the top of a high mountain, where it is further from the center of the earth. The object would also have a different weight on other planets or moons, because the gravitational force there is different than on Earth.

Inertia

Earlier we stated that objects do not move by themselves—a force (a push or a pull) must be applied to make them move. Isaac Newton expressed this idea in more detail: An object at rest (sitting still) will remain at rest and an object in motion will remain in motion at the same speed and in the same direction unless a force acts on it to change the motion. This resistance to a change in motion is known as inertia.

Children can observe the effects of inertia in **Across the Curriculum 6: Safety in Motion**. In this activity the toy vehicle will stop when it hits a solid object, but the unbelted passenger will keep moving. This is because the solid object exerted a force on the vehicle and stopped it, but the force was not exerted on the passenger so it kept moving. When the passenger is "buckled up," the "seat belt" exerts a force on the passenger and stops the passenger from moving separately from the vehicle. This engaging activity not only shows children why seat belts are so important, it can also empower children to talk with family and peers about the science behind seat belts.

Friction

Simply put, friction is the force that prevents things from sliding past each other easily and makes it harder to move things. We've all seen friction at work—it's the force that causes a rolling object to slow down and eventually stop. This is because as the object rolls, irregularities in the object's surface and the surface over which it rolls allow the materials to "grab" one another. The force of this grab is the friction between the object and the surface and it changes depending on the surface that the object is rolling over. Surfaces provide varying amounts of friction. Children will discover that a toy car will roll further on a smooth flooring surface than it will on a carpeted surface. In general, the smoother the surface, the smaller the friction force between the surface and the object. You may want to talk with children about whether they've ever tried to walk on an icy surface—it's difficult to do because ice provides very little friction and a certain amount of friction is necessary for walking.

Wheels

Wheels make moving an object easier and change how things move. Wheels are useful when they turn on axles. As it turns, a wheel exerts a backward force on a surface and the surface exerts a forward force on the wheel. This forward force is what moves the object forward. If the surface is not flexible, the force exerted by the wheel onto the surface is returned to the wheel, maximizing its motion forward. If the surface is flexible (like carpet), the surface moves as the wheel exerts a force on it, so the surface does not return as much force to the wheel and thus there is not as much forward motion by the wheel.

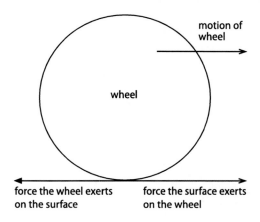

motion of wheel

wheel

force the wheel exerts on the surface

force the surface exerts on the wheel

Ramps and Loops

A ramp is a simple machine that capitalizes on the force of gravity to increase the speed of a rolling object. If you hold a toy car in the air and drop it, it falls to the ground. When you place the same toy car at the top of a ramp and let go, the car rolls down the ramp. In both cases the car moves because the force of gravity acts on it. Children will observe that a toy car rolls farther as the incline of a ramp becomes steeper. This is because the car is moving faster when it reaches the bottom of the ramp. The faster the car is moving when it leaves the ramp, the more distance it can cover before friction slows and stops it.

When a loop is added to the car's track, the fun and the science learning are enhanced. Just before the car enters the loop, it is moving along a straight path. If no new force was exerted on the car, it would continue along this straight path forever. For the car to change direction and start moving in a circle, a force must act on it. As the car enters the loop, a force is exerted against the wheels by the track. For the car to remain in the loop, rather than falling from the track, the car must have enough speed to overcome the force of gravity.

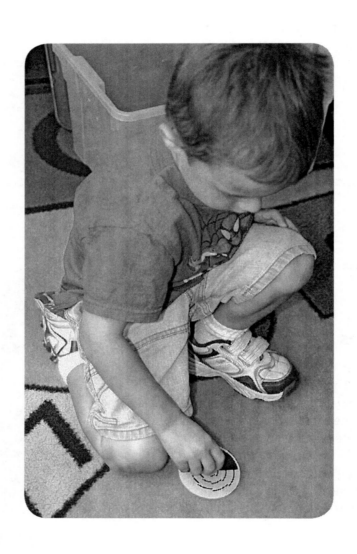

References

American Chemical Society. *Chemistry in the National Science Education Standards: A Reader and Resource Manual for High School Teachers;* Washington, DC, 1997.

Ash, D.; Greene, C.; Austin, M. "Inquiry by Teachers," *Connect.* 2000, *13*(4), 12.

Barman, C.R. "Teaching Teachers: The Learning Cycle," *Science and Children.* 1989, *26*(7), 30–32.

Beisenherz, P.C. "Explore, Invent, and Apply," *Science and Children.* 1991, *28*(4), 30–32.

Bresnik, J. "Facilitating Inquiry," *Connect.* 2000, *13*(4), 6–8.

Chaille, C.; Britain, L. *The Young Child as Scientist: A Constructivist Approach to Early Childhood Science Education;* Allyn & Bacon: Boston, 2003.

Cheong, W. "The Power of Questioning," *Connect.* 2000, *13*(4), 9–10.

Connect: Inquiry Learning Issue. 1995, *8*(4), 1–20.

Connect: Inquiry Learning Issue. 2000, *13*(4), 1–26.

Dialogue on Early Childhood Science, Mathematics, and Technology Education; American Association for the Advancement of Science (AAAS) Project 2061: Washington, DC, 1999.

Eager to Learn: Educating Our Preschoolers; Bowman, B.T., Donovan, S.M., Burns, M.S., Eds.; National Academy Press: Washington, DC, 2001.

Edwards, C.; Gandini, L.; Forman, G. *The Hundred Languages of Children: The Reggio Emilia Approach to Early Childhood Education;* Ablex Publishing Corporation: Norwood, NJ, 1993.

Gandini, L. "Fundamentals of the Reggio Emilia Approach to Early Childhood Education," *Young Children.* 1993, *49*(1), 4–8.

Helm, J.; Beneke, S.; Steinheimer, K. *Windows on Learning: Documenting Young Children's Work;* Teachers College Press: New York, 1998.

Hoisington, C. "Using Photographs to Support Children's Science Inquiry," *Young Children.* 2002, *57*(5), 26–32.

Jones, J.; Courtney, R. "Documenting Early Science Learning," *Young Children.* 2002, *57*(5), 34–40.

Katz, L. "Impressions of Reggio Emilia Preschools," *Young Children*. 1990, *45*(6), 10–11.

Katz, L.G.; Chard, S.C. *The Contribution of Documentation to the Quality of Early Childhood Education*. ERIC/EECE Clearinghouse on Elementary and Early Childhood Education, 1996. www.ericdigests.org/1996-4/quality.htm (accessed January 24, 2008).

Kilmer, S.J.; Hofman, H. "Transforming Science Curriculum," *Reaching Potentials: Transforming Early Childhood Curriculum and Assessment,* Vol. 2; National Association for the Education of Young Children: Washington, DC, 1995: pp 43–63.

Lind, K. *Exploring Science in Early Childhood: A Developmental Approach;* Delmar Publishers: Albany, NY, 2000.

Lind, K. "Science in Early Childhood: Developing and Acquiring Fundamental Concepts and Skills." Dialogue on Early Childhood Science, Mathematics, and Technology Education. American Association for the Advancement of Science (AAAS), 1999.

Lowery, L. *The Biological Basis of Thinking and Learning;* Lawrence Hall of Science: Berkeley, CA, 1998.

Lowery, L. "How New Science Curriculums Reflect Brain Research," *Educational Leadership*. 1998, *56*(3), 26–30.

Lowery, L. *The Scientific Thinking Process;* Lawrence Hall of Science: Berkeley, CA, 1992.

Marek, E.A.; Cavallo, A.M.L. *The Learning Cycle: Elementary School Science and Beyond;* Heinemann: Portsmouth, NH, 1997.

Meisels, S.J., et al. *An Overview: The Work Sampling System;* Rebus Planning Associates: Ann Arbor, MI, 1994.

Moriarty, R. "Entries from a Staff Developer's Journal...Helping Teachers Develop as Facilitators of Three- to Five-Year-Olds' Science Inquiry," *Young Children*. 2002, *57*(5), 20–24.

National Association for the Education of Young Children (NAEYC). *Developmentally Appropriate Practice in Early Childhood Programs Serving Children from Birth through Age 8,* 1997. www.naeyc.org/about/positions/daptoc.asp (accessed January 31, 2008).

National Association for the Education of Young Children (NAEYC). *Guidelines for Appropriate Curriculum Content and Assessment in Programs Serving Children Ages 3 through 8.* Produced jointly with NAECS/SDE and NAEYC and adopted by both Associations in 1990. Published in *Young Children,* March 1991, pp 21–38 and in *Reaching Potentials: Appropriate Curriculum and Assessment for Young Children,* Volume 1, 1991, pp 9–27. *naecs.crc.uiuc.edu/position/currcont.html* (accessed September 9, 2008).

National Research Council. *National Science Education Standards: Observe, Interact, Change, Learn;* National Academy Press: Washington, DC, 1996.

Reaching Potentials: Appropriate Curriculum and Assessment for Young Children, Vol. 1. Bredekamp, S., Rosegrant, T., Eds. Washington, DC: National Association for the Education of Young Children (NAEYC), 1992.

Reaching Potentials: Appropriate Curriculum and Assessment for Young Children, Vol. 2. Bredekamp, S., Rosegrant, T., Eds. Washington, DC: National Association for the Education of Young Children (NAEYC), 1995.

Taylor, B.A.P.; Poth, J.; Portman, D.J. *Teaching Physics with TOYS;* Terrific Science: Middletown, OH, 1995.

Taylor, B.A.P.; Portman, D.J.; Gertz, S.; Hogue, L. *Teaching Physics with TOYS, EASYGuide Edition;* Terrific Science: Middletown, OH, 2005.

Villavicencio, J. "Inquiry in Kindergarten," *Connect.* 2000, *13*(4), 3–5.

Lightning Source UK Ltd.
Milton Keynes UK
UKOW041314141211

183781UK00004B/7/P